Getting Skills Right

Continuous Learning in Working Life in Finland

This work is published under the responsibility of the Secretary-General of the OECD. The opinions expressed and arguments employed herein do not necessarily reflect the official views of OECD member countries.

This document, as well as any data and map included herein, are without prejudice to the status of or sovereignty over any territory, to the delimitation of international frontiers and boundaries and to the name of any territory, city or area.

The statistical data for Israel are supplied by and under the responsibility of the relevant Israeli authorities. The use of such data by the OECD is without prejudice to the status of the Golan Heights, East Jerusalem and Israeli settlements in the West Bank under the terms of international law.

Please cite this publication as:
OECD (2020), *Continuous Learning in Working Life in Finland*, Getting Skills Right, OECD Publishing, Paris, *https://doi.org/10.1787/2ffcffe6-en*.

ISBN 978-92-64-87262-2 (print)
ISBN 978-92-64-63549-4 (pdf)

Getting Skills Right
ISSN 2520-6117 (print)
ISSN 2520-6125 (online)

Photo credits: Cover Cell phone: © Creative Commons/Alfredo Hernandez, clock: © Creative Commons/Hakan Yalcin, cloud upload: Creative Commons/Warslab, join: © Creative Commons/Tom Ingebretsen, doctor: © Creative Commons/Joseph Wilson, chef: © Creative Commons/Alfonso Melolontha.

Corrigenda to publications may be found on line at: *www.oecd.org/about/publishing/corrigenda.htm*.
© OECD 2020

The use of this work, whether digital or print, is governed by the Terms and Conditions to be found at *http://www.oecd.org/termsandconditions*.

Foreword

The world of work is changing. Digitalisation, globalisation, and population ageing are having a profound impact on the type and quality of jobs that are available and the skills required to perform them. The extent to which individuals, firms and economies can reap the benefits of these changes will depend critically on the readiness of adult learning systems to help people develop and maintain relevant skills over their working careers.

To explore this issue, the OECD Directorate for Employment, Labour and Social Affairs has undertaken an ambitious programme of work on the functioning, effectiveness and resilience of adult learning systems across countries. This includes the creation of the Priorities for Adult Learning (PAL) dashboard for comparing the readiness of each country's adult learning system to address future skills challenges, as well as a cross-country report, *Getting Skills Right: Future-Ready Adult Learning Systems*, which showcases relevant policy examples from OECD and emerging countries. The Directorate is also carrying out a series of in-depth country reviews of adult learning systems to offer a comprehensive analysis of the key areas where policy action is required.

This report on *Continuous Learning in Working Life in Finland* was prepared by Anja Meierkord and Anna Vindics from the Skills and Employability Division of the Directorate for Employment, Labour and Social Affairs under the supervision of Glenda Quintini (Skills team manager) and Mark Keese (Head of the Skills and Employability Division). Helpful comments were provided by Stefano Scarpetta (Director for Employment, Labour and Social Affairs), as well as Alessia Forti and Katherine Mullock (Skills and Employability Division).

The report benefited greatly from discussions with Finnish experts, officials, employer federations, trade unions, academics and education institutions during two missions of the OECD team to Finland in March and July 2019. It also profited from comments by participants in a validation workshop organised in Helsinki in November 2019 and written comments to the draft version provided by the Ministry of Education and Culture and the Ministry of Economic Affairs and Employment. Special thanks are given to Petri Haltia (Ministry of Education and Culture), Kirsi Heinivirta (Ministry of Education and Culture), Kimmo Ruth (Ministry of Economic Affairs and Employment) and Aleksi Kalenius (formerly Permanent Delegation for Finland to the OECD and UNESCO).

This report is published under the responsibility of the Secretary General of the OECD, with the financial assistance of the Finnish Ministry of Education and Culture and the Finnish Ministry of Economic Affairs and Employment. The views expressed in this report should not be taken to reflect the official position of OECD member countries.

Table of contents

Foreword	3
Acronyms and abbreviations	7
Executive summary	8
Assessment and recommendations	10
1 The changing policy context	**13**
Introduction	14
Labour market context	15
Skill levels of the adult population	20
Patterns of adult learning participation	23
References	28
Notes	30
2 The continuous learning system	**31**
Introduction	32
Governance	32
Financing	33
Structure of provision	37
References	39
3 Making continuous learning provision fit for the future	**40**
Introduction	41
The current system	41
Key challenges	50
Policy recommendations and good practices	54
References	64
Notes	69
4 Improving learning participation of adults with low skills	**70**
Introduction	71
The current situation	72
Key challenges	84
Policy recommendations and good practices	88
References	94

FIGURES

Figure 1.1. Protracted recovery from the economic crisis	15
Figure 1.2. A labour market on the upswing	16
Figure 1.3. Job creation is skill-biased in Finland	17
Figure 1.4. Pronounced shortages in high-skilled occupations in international comparison	18
Figure 1.5. Jobs at risk of automation	19
Figure 1.6. A decreasing working age population	20
Figure 1.7. Information-processing skills are some of the highest in the OECD	21
Figure 1.8. A decreasing share of younger adults are obtaining tertiary degrees	22
Figure 1.9. The group of potential adult learners is diverse	22
Figure 1.10. More than half of Finnish adults participate in job-related learning	23
Figure 1.11. Time trends of participation provide a mixed-picture depending on data source	24
Figure 1.12. Learning intensity in Finland is high	25
Figure 1.13. There are large participation gaps between groups	26
Figure 1.14. Inverse trends in Finland and the EU-28 in the importance of different forms of training	26
Figure 1.15. A high share of adult learners are young adults in formal education	27
Figure 2.1. Government is key funder of adult learning	34
Figure 2.2. Investment in adult learning is high by international comparison	36
Figure 2.3. Public investment is high, while company investment is lagging behind	36
Figure 3.1. Self-motivated studies are now dominating the ALMP training offer	46
Figure 3.2. Adults increasingly pursue bachelor degrees at UAS	50
Figure 3.3. Participation in formal and informal adult learning are associated with lower wages	53
Figure 4.1. The share of adults with low basic skills is comparatively small in Finland	72
Figure 4.2. Adults with low basic skills are typically older, from low socio-economic background and/or migrants	73
Figure 4.3. A high share of adults with low skills are inactive	74
Figure 4.4. Adults with low level of basic skills tend to work at smaller private sector companies	75
Figure 4.5. Low-skilled adults are overrepresented in sectors with more manual and routine jobs	75
Figure 4.6. Participation gap between low and medium/high skilled adults is largest in the OECD	76
Figure 4.7. Many adults with low skills neither participate nor do they want to	77
Figure 4.8. Many adults with low basic skills participate in learning because they have to	78
Figure 4.9. The participation rate of low-skilled employed adults in Finland is comparatively high	79
Figure 4.10. Employers in Finland frequently cover training cost of adults with low basic skills	79
Figure 4.11. Adults with low basic skills do not participate in the ALMPs that yield the best outcomes for them	80
Figure 4.12. Barriers to participation differ between low and higher skilled adults	85
Figure 4.13. Very few Finnish adults with low basic skills take part in formal education.	86
Figure 4.14. Adults with low skills are less likely to seek out information on learning opportunities	87

TABLES

Table 1.1. Many shortage occupations are high skilled	17
Table 2.1. Types of formal and non-formal adult learning provision in Finland	37
Table 2.2. Types of education providers involved in the delivery of adult learning in Finland	38
Table 3.1. Types of basic and general adult education provision in Finland	41
Table 3.2. Types of adult vocational education in Finland	42
Table 3.3. Types of adult higher education in Finland	44
Table 3.4. Types of adult liberal education in Finland	44
Table 3.5. Types of staff training in Finland	45

Follow OECD Publications on:

- http://twitter.com/OECD_Pubs
- http://www.facebook.com/OECDPublications
- http://www.linkedin.com/groups/OECD-Publications-4645871
- http://www.youtube.com/oecdilibrary
- http://www.oecd.org/oecddirect/

Acronyms and abbreviations

AES	Adult Education Survey
AI	Artificial Intelligence
ALMP	Active Labour Market Policy
CVTS	Continuing Vocational Training Survey
ECTS	European Credit Transfer System
EDUFIN	Finnish National Agency for Education
EIB	European Investment Bank
ELY	Centres for Economic Development, Transport and the Environment
EU	European Union
EQF	European Qualification Framework
FiNQF	Finnish Qualification Framework
GDP	Gross Domestic Product
IALS	Adult Literacy Survey
ISCED	International Standard Classification of Education
ISCO	International Standard Classification of Occupations
IVET	Initial Vocational Education and Training
LFS	Labour Force Survey
OECD	Organisation for Economic Cooperation and Development
MoEC	Ministry of Education and Culture Finland
MoEE	Ministry of Economic Affairs and Employment Finland
MoF	Ministry of Finance
MoI	Ministry of Interior
MoSAH	Ministry of Social Affairs and Health
PES	Public Employment Services
PIAAC	OECD Survey of Adult Skills
PISA	Programme for International Student Assessment
TE	Employment and Economic Development offices, Finnish public employment services
TYP	Multi-Sectoral Joint Services Centres
UAS	University of Applied Sciences

Executive summary

Finland's skill development system is one of the most successful in the OECD. The country's 15-year old students have been amongst the top performers of all the countries participating in the Programme for International Student Assessment (PISA) since its first edition in 2000. Its adult population has some of the highest levels of literacy and numeracy in the OECD, according to the OECD Survey of Adult Skills (PIAAC), surpassed only by Japan. Large shares of the population continue learning over the life-course, as two in three adults participate in formal or non-formal learning activities every year.

To maintain these remarkable performances, the skill development system needs to adapt to a rapidly changing labour market. Globalisation, technological change and population ageing are affecting the types of jobs that are and will be available in Finland and how they are carried out. As the vast majority of people affected by these changes are already in the labour market, addressing the skills of the existing workforce will be key to managing the transition. Giving adults better opportunities to upskill and reskill will improve their economic outcomes and well-being, as well as help maintain the competitiveness of Finnish firms and the economy as a whole.

This report assesses the current system of continuous learning in working life in Finland, i.e. the system of job-related learning of adults who have completed their initial education and entered working life. Two specific aspects of the system were selected for in-depth review: i) the structure of adult learning provision, meaning the set of learning opportunities available to adults, as well as their alignment with labour market needs; ii) the inclusiveness of the system towards adults with low skills.

In these areas, the report identifies the following key challenges:

- There are some gaps in learning provision, including limited upskilling opportunities for adults with vocational qualifications and, more generally, limited availability of short courses relevant to the labour market.
- The current financial incentive system leads to inefficiencies by encouraging participation in formal education, such as bachelor degrees, rather than non-formal or informal learning, such as participation in seminars and learning from peers.
- The existing education and training provision has limited alignment with labour market needs, not least due to the lack of strong mechanisms to use skill anticipation information in policymaking.
- Finland has the largest gaps in learning participation between adults with low basic skills and those with higher skill levels amongst OECD economies, as it offers little targeted support for adults with low skills, be this outreach activities, advice and guidance services or specific training programmes.

To address these challenges, the report makes the following recommendations:

- **Develop an overarching vision for the continuous learning system** and a strategy about how different types of provision contribute to the whole.
- **Diversify the training offer** by i) considering the expansion of non-formal learning opportunities and improving the market for such provision; ii) reintroducing opportunities to develop higher

vocational skills (EQF-level 6); and iii) exploring the introduction of short-cycle tertiary education in selected subject-areas.
- **Make training offers more labour market relevant** through i) systematising the use of skill assessment and anticipation information for strategic planning; ii) harnessing the capacity of employers to develop training programmes; and iii) incentivising providers to offer training in line with skill demand by strengthening the link between funding and the content of training courses.
- **Incentivise individuals to engage in labour-market relevant training** by i) providing better information on the labour market relevance of training; and ii) reviewing and calibrating financial incentives in order to address the current bias of the incentive structure towards participation in formal education, and introducing incentives for individuals to take-up training for skills in demand.
- **Provide comprehensive information and guidance services for the low-skilled**, notably through i) strengthening the capacity of TE-offices to deliver comprehensive career advice and guidance to adults with low skills; and ii) developing physical one-stop guidance services for adults with low skills addressing the complexity of their barriers to training.
- **Develop tailored education programmes for the low skilled** that aim to improve motivation towards learning and link to everyday aspects of their lives, such as their workplace, community or role as parents.
- **Reach out to adults with low skills** by means of i) funding outreach activities through trade unions, NGOs or members of the group themselves; and ii) improving the understanding of the target group by collecting and analysing data on its characteristics, participation patterns and outcomes.

This report encompasses four chapters: Chapter 1 sets out the changing policy context for skills policy in Finland. It discusses changes in skill demand and supply, as well as patterns of participation in adult learning opportunities. Chapter 2 presents information on the basic features of the current system of continuous learning in working life, how it is governed and financed. Chapter 3 provides an in-depth analysis of the current structure of the adult learning provision, as well as its alignment with the changing skill needs of the labour market. Chapter 4 assesses the situation of adults with low skills in the continuous learning system, reviewing their participation patterns and the learning provision available to them. Both Chapter 3 and 4 highlight the key challenges arising from the current situation and make recommendations on how to tackle these, based on international evidence.

Assessment and recommendations

Assessment

Finland's skill development system is one of the most successful in the OECD. The country's 15-year old students have been amongst the top performers of all the countries participating in the Programme for International Student Assessment (PISA) since its first edition in 2000. Its adult population has some of the highest levels of literacy and numeracy in the OECD, according to the OECD Survey of Adult Skills (PIAAC), surpassed only by Japan.

To maintain these remarkable performances, the skill development system needs to adapt to a rapidly changing labour market. Globalisation, technological change and population ageing are affecting the types of jobs that are and will be available in Finland and how they are carried out. Today, the vast majority of new jobs created require high levels of skills, while meta-cognitive and digital skills are becoming more important in working life. Skill shortages in the Finnish labour market are increasingly apparent and there are growing concerns about the supply of higher-level skills, given demographic change and stagnating, albeit high, educational attainment levels.

Finland's skill development system must get future-ready. As the vast majority of people affected by these changes are already in the labour market, addressing the skills of the existing workforce will be key to managing the transition. Giving adults better opportunities to upskill and reskill will improve their economic outcomes and well-being, as well as maintain the competitiveness of Finnish firms and the economy as a whole.

Finland starts from a good basis. Its adult learning system is well developed and offers a wide range of learning opportunities at all skill levels. More than one in two adults participate in job-related learning activities every year – a high share in international comparisons. However, participation is unevenly distributed in the population and especially low amongst adults with low-skills, the long-term unemployed, as well as older adults. The current system could also be calibrated better to help all adults keep abreast with the transformation of the labour market. The report identifies the following challenges:

1. Some gaps in learning provision, including limited upskilling opportunities for adults with vocational qualifications and, more generally, limited availability of short courses relevant to the labour market.
2. A financial incentive system that leads to inefficiencies by encouraging participation in formal education, such as bachelor degrees, rather than non-formal or informal learning, such as participation in seminars and learning from peers.
3. The limited alignment of existing education and training provision with labour market needs, not least due to the lack of strong mechanisms to use skill anticipation information in policymaking.

What is more, Finland has the largest gaps in learning participation between adults with low basic skills and those with higher skill levels amongst OECD economies. This is problematic, as the employment opportunities for low-skilled adults are shrinking. Barriers to accessing learning provision are already low in Finland, with much of the provision being offered for free or at a low-cost to the individual, delivered flexibly and in principle being open to adults at all skill levels. However, given the universal nature of Finnish adult learning provision it offers little targeted support for adults with low skills, be this outreach activities, advice and guidance services or specific training programmes. This is an issue, as more than half of all adults with low skills in Finland do not wish to take up education opportunities at all. Attitudinal barriers play an important role in this, such as undervaluing the benefits of education and training, negative experiences with initial education or network effects, notably the low training participation of their peer group. Offering more targeted support for adults with low basic skills to upskill or reskill is now becoming an economic imperative for a future of work that is more inclusive and productive.

Recommendations

The report develops in-depth recommendations in two specific areas. Firstly, it suggests that Finland must improve the future-readiness of the structure of its provision. Secondly, it proposes that Finland must improve the learning participation of adults with low skills. The system would also benefit from reforms in the areas of governance and financing of adult learning, as well as a review of incentives emanating from the social security system, although these were not the explicit subject of this report. Hence, Finland should consider to:

- *Develop an overarching vision for the continuous learning system* and a strategy about how different types of provision contribute to the whole. This should also include a review of the linkages between the adult learning system and other policy areas such as initial education or the social security system. Work in this area has already commenced and suggestions for a comprehensive reform of the continuous learning system are expected by the end of 2020.

Making continuous learning provision fit for the future

To give adults the best possible opportunities to reskill and upskill for a changing world of work, the Finnish adult learning system should close some gaps in the learning offer, make the offer more labour market relevant and incentivise individuals to take-part in labour market relevant training.

Diversify the training offer

- *Consider the expansion of non-formal learning opportunities* and improve the market for such provision. This must go hand-in-hand with the development of quality assurance mechanisms for new learning opportunities, such as the accreditation and certification of providers and programmes.
- *Reintroduce opportunities to develop higher vocational skills* (EQF-level 6) to expand upskilling opportunities for adults whose highest educational qualification is a vocational degree and who wish to pursue further vocational qualifications. This could also help to alleviate some of the pressure on the higher education system, providing alternatives to bachelor degree study at Universities of Applied Sciences for this target group.
- *Explore the introduction of short-cycle tertiary education* in selected subject-areas to diversify the number of learning options at tertiary level and provide opportunities for those who do not have the time or inclination to take part in lengthy Bachelor degree courses. These tertiary level degree courses would take between one and two years to complete. This could also reduce some of the pressures on the higher education system, as the recommendation above.

Make training offers more labour market relevant

- *Systematise the use of skill assessment and anticipation information for strategic planning* and use the ongoing parliamentary reform on continuous learning as an opportunity to review current practices in this area.
- *Harness the capacity of employers to develop training programmes,* for example by introducing employer-led sectoral committees to develop labour market relevant non-formal learning provision.
- *Incentivise providers to offer training in line with skill demand* by strengthening the link between funding and the content of training courses.

Incentivise individuals to engage in labour-market relevant training

- *Provide better information on the labour market relevance of training,* notably through a comprehensive online information portal, which brings together information on course availability, participant outcomes and satisfaction, as well as more general information on skills and occupational labour market demand.
- *Review and calibrate financial incentives in order* to: i) address the current bias of the incentive structure towards participation in formal education; and ii) introduce incentives for individuals to take-up training for skills in demand.

Improving learning participation of adults with low skills

Finland's adult learning system should take into account the specific needs of adults with low skills and develop appropriate policy responses.

Provide comprehensive information and guidance services

- *Strengthen the capacity of TE-offices to deliver comprehensive career advice and guidance to adults with low skills*, including through training of guidance staff and increasing funding for the public employment services, which have experienced significant budget cuts over the past decade.
- *Additionally, develop physical one-stop guidance services for adults with low skills addressing the complexity of their barriers to training.* Consider streamlining these services with existing one-stop shops for specific target groups (i.e. youth, adults with a migrant background, the long-term unemployed).

Develop tailored education programmes

- *Develop a programme of short courses tailored to adults with low basic skills that aim to improve motivation towards learning.* These 'taster courses' can provide an entryway to rekindle their interest towards learning and should have limited emphasis on learning outcomes, grading or exams. They would *provide contextualised learning,* linked to everyday aspects of adults' lives, such as their workplace, community or their role as parents

Reach out to adults with low basic skills

- *Fund outreach activities for adults with low basic skills* through trade unions, NGOs or members of the group themselves.
- *Improve understanding of the target group* by collecting and analysing data on its characteristics, participation patterns and outcomes.

1 The changing policy context

After years of lacklustre economic performance, Finland has seen a strong improvement of its labour market conditions since 2016. Its future economic prospects will depend on the readiness of its continuous learning system to respond to the changing skill needs of the labour market. In the context of globalisation, technological progress and demographic change, the demand for high-level skills is growing and skill imbalances are starting to intensify. There are concerns in how far the high skill levels of the Finnish population can be maintained and further increased to address these changes. This chapter discusses how skill demand and supply are changing in Finland, as well as arising skill imbalances. It concludes that Finland can build on high participation in continuous learning to address these changes, but some groups are at risk of being left behind.

Introduction

Finland's skill development system is one of the most successful in the OECD. The country's 15-year old students have been amongst the top performers of all the countries participating in the Programme for International Student Assessment (PISA) since its first edition in 2000. Its adult population has some of the highest levels of literacy and numeracy in the OECD, according to the OECD Survey of Adult Skills (PIAAC), surpassed only by Japan. Large shares of the population continue learning over the life-course, as two in three adults participate in formal or non-formal learning activities every year.

Yet, the skills needed in the labour market are changing. Globalisation, technological change and population ageing are affecting the types of jobs that are available in Finland and how they are carried out. National and international research shows that the level of skills needed to obtain and maintain jobs is rising, meta-cognitive skills, such as learning to learn, are becoming more important and advanced technology use is becoming omnipresent in working life. This review comes at a time when skill shortages in the Finnish labour market are becoming increasingly apparent and there are growing concerns about the supply of high-level skills, given demographic change and stagnating educational attainment levels. To maintain its position as one of the world's foremost knowledge economies, Finland's skill development system must adapt to these changes in the labour market.

Managing these changes starts with investment in early childhood and initial education to equip young people with strong foundation skills for a changing world of work. However, it may take 10-25 years for these investments to translate into changes in the supply of skills in the labour market; far too long given the current pace of change if the Finish economy is to remain competitive. As the vast majority of people affected by these changes are already in the labour market, addressing the skills of the existing workforce will be key to managing the transition. Giving adults the opportunity to upskill and reskill will support their economic outcomes and well-being, as well as maintain the competitiveness of Finnish firms and the economy as a whole.

Box 1.1. Defining continuous learning

This report focuses on continuous learning in working life. This includes job-related learning of adults, who have completed their initial education and entered working life. Job-related learning refers to education and training that is being undertaken for the purpose of gaining skills for a current or future job, while acknowledging that non-job related 'recreational' learning can also provide individuals with valuable skills for the labour market.

One can further distinguish between three types of continuous learning: formal and non-formal education and training, as well as informal learning (Eurostat, 2016[1]):

- **Formal education** are intentional, institutionalised learning activities, which are recognised by the relevant authorities and have a minimum duration of one semester.
- **Non-formal education** are intentional, institutionalised learning activities, e.g. short-courses, workshops or seminars, which are either of short duration (less than one semester) or not recognised by the relevant authorities.
- **Informal learning** is intentional, non-institutionalised, less structured and can take place anywhere, e.g. when learning from colleagues, friends or learning by doing.

In the following, individuals who engage in continuous learning in working life are referred to as adult learners. Continuous learning in working life, continuous learning, adult learning and adult education and training are used interchangeably to refer to learning opportunities for this group.

Labour market context

Having been hit hard by the global financial and economic crisis, Finland experienced an extended period of lacklustre economic performance over the past decade (OECD, 2018[2]). In the past two years, the economy has regained momentum and, in 2018, the employment rate hit 72% for the first time on record. Yet, the new jobs that are being created are not the same as those lost during the crisis. The interlinked challenges of globalisation, technological progress and population ageing are changing the type of jobs that are available in Finland and how they are carried out. Today, the majority of new jobs are emerging in high-skilled occupations, be it in the thriving technology sector, education or high-skilled care professions.

Following a protracted recovery, the Finnish employment rate is at an all-time high...

Finland's economy has only recently strengthened, following a near-decade of low economic growth. The impact of the global economic crisis hit Finland harder than many other OECD economies (Figure 1.1). GDP growth plummeted to -8% in 2009, compared with smaller declines in the Nordic neighbour economies Norway (-2%) and Sweden (-5%). The economy entered a short period of recovery in 2010/2011, but was hit by major economic challenges in its electronic, paper and forest industries, as well as a severe economic recession in Russia from 2014, one of its major trading partners (OECD, 2018[2]; OECD, 2016[3]; OECD, 2014[4]; OECD, 2012[5]). Finland fell back into a protracted recession between 2012 and 2014 and returned to economic growth only in 2015. Since then, the economy has seen robust growth, outperforming other OECD and Nordic economies. Economic expansion is projected to continue in the coming two years, albeit at a slower pace than previously (OECD, 2019[6]). Overall, Finland's GDP remains lower per capita than in other Nordic countries, primarily due to lower productivity and labour utilisation (OECD, 2018[1]).

Figure 1.1. Protracted recovery from the economic crisis

Annual real GDP growth, percentage, 2005-2018

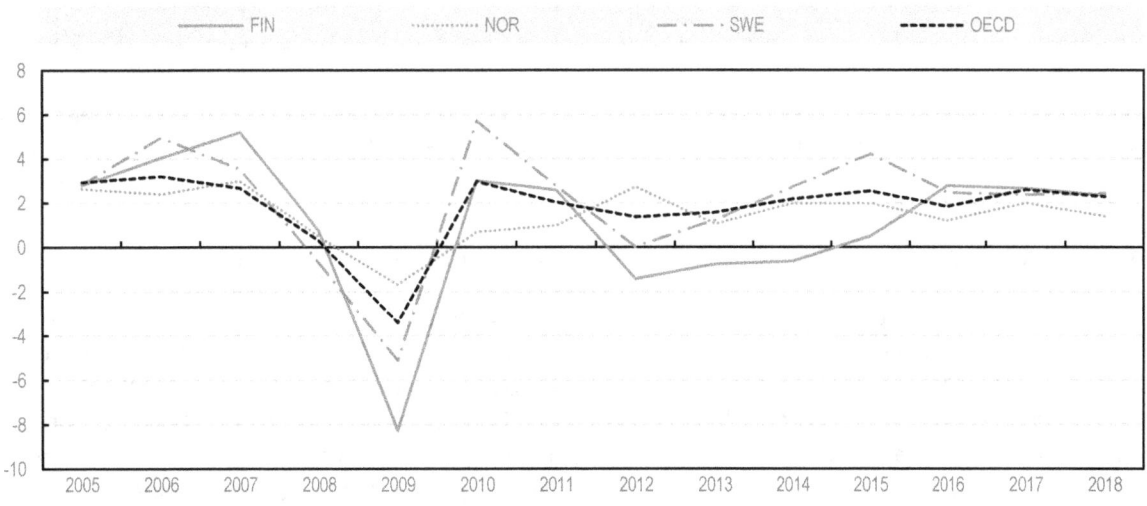

Source: OECD National Accounts database.

Finland's economic performance over the past decade is mirrored in the labour market. Employment rates dropped to 68% in the last quarter of 2009 from a peak of 71% in the second quarter of 2008; a decrease equivalent to close to 100 000 people (Figure 1.2). After years of stalling growth, the employment rate has steadily increased since 2017, surpassing 72% in the second quarter of 2018, which is the highest rate on record. However, a substantial gap between Finland and its Nordic neighbours, Norway (Q2 2019: 75%) and Sweden (Q2 2019: 77%), remains.

The new government has set an ambitious employment rate target of 75% (Finnish Government, 2019[7]), which will require structural reforms to activate the so far unrealised potential of the population. Total unemployment is already close to the estimated structural unemployment levels. Growth could come through speeding up young people's labour market entry (OECD, 2019[8]), delaying the labour market exit of older workers, raising participation of women with small children, addressing labour market imbalances, and strengthening work incentives and activation policies more widely (OECD, 2018[2]). The latter is especially important, given the comparatively high unemployment rates in Finland. While the unemployment rate is now close to pre-crisis levels (Q2 2019: 7%), it remains above the OECD average (5%) and the rate of Norway (3%) (Figure 1.2).

Figure 1.2. A labour market on the upswing

Quarterly employment and harmonised unemployment rates, percentage, Q1 2005-Q2 2019

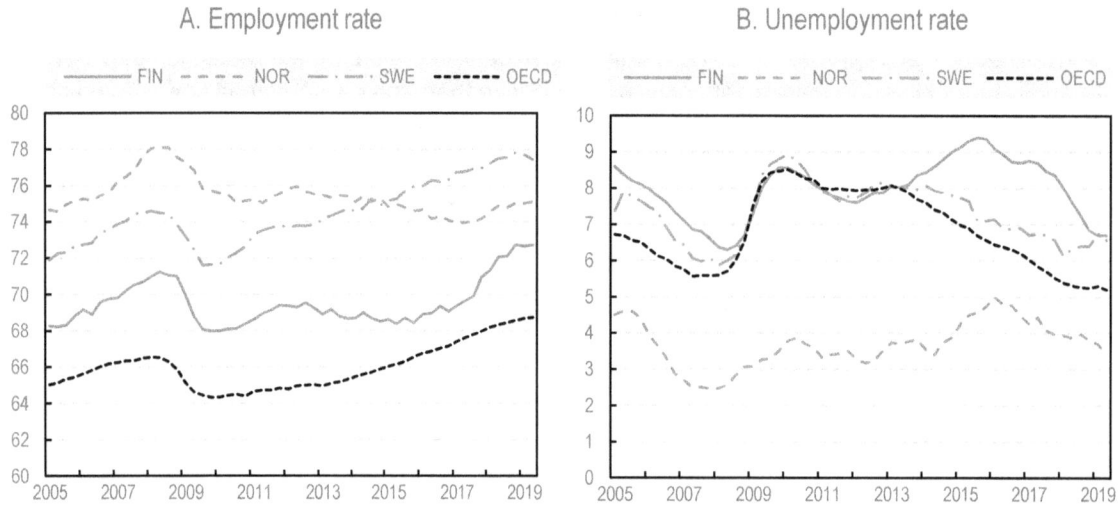

Note: Employment rate as percentage of population aged 15-64, seasonally adjusted; harmonised unemployment rate as percentage of people of working age who are without work, are available for work, and have taken specific steps to find work, of the labour force.
Source: OECD Labour Market Statistics.

...and the vast majority of new jobs created require high levels of skills.

As employment in Finland continues to grow, it is becoming clear that the new jobs are in different sectors than in the past and require different skill-sets. According to data from Statistics Finland, employment in the service sector grew by more than 5% in the past decade alone, while employment in agriculture and manufacturing decreased by 15% and 11% respectively.[1] New employment opportunities over the past decades (1998-2018) have overwhelmingly required high-level skills, while growth in the low-skilled occupations was more modest and middle-skilled jobs were displaced. It is worth noting that compared to other Nordic countries, Finland has seen higher growth of jobs in low-skilled occupations in the past two decades, and in recent years more specifically (Figure 1.3).

Figure 1.3. Job creation is skill-biased in Finland

Percentage point change in share of total employment, 1998 to 2018

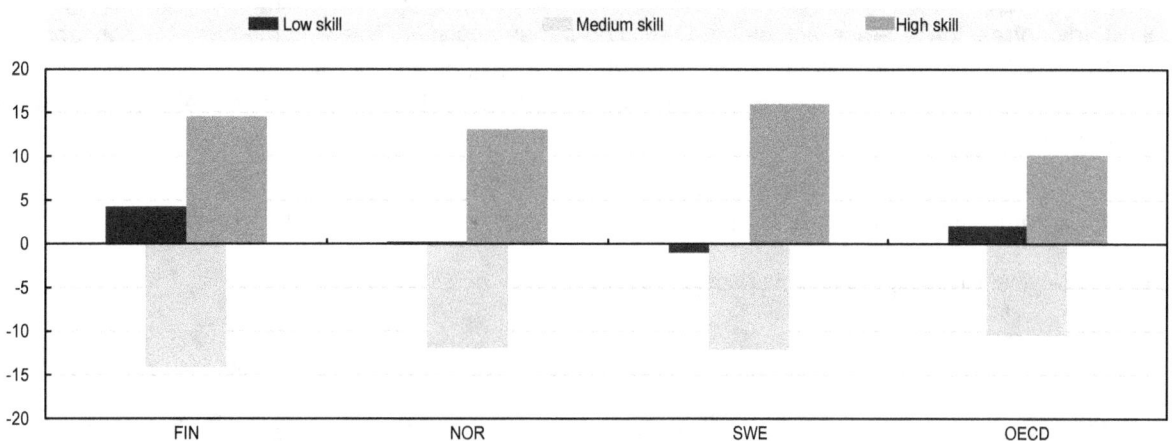

Note: High-skilled jobs correspond to ISCO-88 major groups 1, 2, and 3; Middle-skilled jobs correspond to ISCO-88 major groups 4, 6, 7 and 8; and low-skilled jobs correspond to ISCO-88 major groups 5 and 9. OECD average is a simple unweighted average of selected OECD countries:
Source: Update of OECD (2017[9]): "How technology and globalisation are transforming the labour market", in *OECD Employment Outlook 2017*, https://doi.org/10.1787/empl_outlook-2017-7-en, based on data from the European and national labour force surveys.

These developments have translated into imbalances in the Finnish labour market. According to the most recent occupational barometer by the Finnish Ministry of Economic Affairs and Employment (*Ammattibarometri*), 52 occupations were in shortage in the second half of 2019, more than twice the number of occupations than only two years earlier, but slightly down from the first half of 2019 (Ministry of Economic Affairs and Employment, 2019[10]; Ministry of Economic Affairs and Employment, 2019[11]). Among the top 15 occupations in shortage, there are many high-skilled occupations in health care and education professions, such as social work and counselling professionals, medical practitioners and early childhood educators (Table 1.1). The list also features several middle and low-skilled professions.

Table 1.1. Many shortage occupations are high skilled

Top and bottom 15 occupations by labour market demand, H2 2019

Top 15 shortage occupations	Top 15 surplus occupations
Social Work and Counselling Professionals	Secretaries (general)
Early Childhood Educators	Tailors, Dressmakers, Furriers and Hatters
Cleaners and Helpers in Offices, Hotels and Other Establishments	Graphic and Multimedia Designers
Audiologists and Speech Therapists	Information and Communication Technology Installers and Servicers
Generalist Medical Practitioners	Information and Communications Technology User Support Technicians
Specialist Medical Practitioners	Journalists
Nursing Associate Professionals	Administrative and Executive Secretaries
Health Care Assistants	Advertising and Marketing Professionals
Contact Centre Salespersons	Cabinet-makers and Related Workers
Cooks	Printers
Commercial Sales Representatives	Pre-press Technicians
Dentists	Sociologists, Anthropologists and Related Professions
Special Needs Teachers	Woodworking Machine Tool Setters and Operators
Psychologists	Library Clerks
Domestic Cleaners and Helpers	Product and Garment Designers

Note: Based on assessments of TE offices regarding short-term skill demands.
Source: Ministry of Employment and the Economy (2019), *Occupational Barometer*, https://www.ammattibarometri.fi/?kieli=en.

Finland stands out in international comparisons for the concentration of shortages in high-skilled occupations. According to the OECD Skills for Jobs database, more than 9 in 10 jobs in shortage in Finland were in high skilled occupations such as managerial or professional occupations (Figure 1.4) – the highest share of shortages in predominantly high-skilled occupations across all countries analysed (OECD, 2018[12]). In contrast, on average across the OECD countries analysed, this was the case for only about 5 out of 10 jobs in shortage. Instead, approximately 4 in 10 jobs in shortage were in medium-skilled occupations, such as sales or handicraft workers, and 1 in 10 jobs in shortage were in low-skilled elementary professions.

Figure 1.4. Pronounced shortages in high-skilled occupations in international comparison

Share of employment in occupations in shortage by skill level, 2015

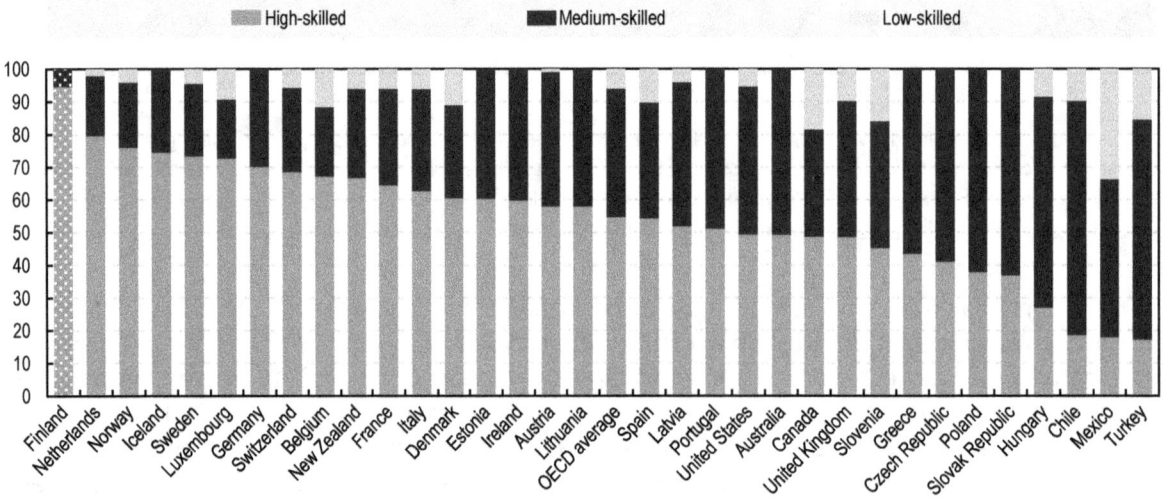

Note: High, medium and low skilled occupations are ISCO occupational groups 1 to 3, 4 to 8 and 9 respectively. Shares of employment in each skill tier are computed as the corresponding employment in each group over the total number of workers in shortage in each country. Data refer to the latest year for which information is available: AUS (2016), DEU (2012), ILS (2013), MEX (2016), NZL (2017), NOR (2014), SVN (2012), USA (2017)
Source: OECD (2018[12]), Skills for Jobs, https://www.oecdskillsforjobsdatabase.org/data/Skills%20SfJ_PDF%20for%20WEBSITE%20final.pdf, based on the OECD Skills for Jobs database (2018).

Technological progress will induce further changes in the labour market…

State-of-the-art technologies, such as artificial intelligence or industrial robotics, are increasingly able to perform many of the tasks traditionally done by human labour. These technologies have the positive effect of enabling workers to focus on less routine, safer and more productive tasks, as well as giving consumers access to more and higher quality goods and services (OECD, 2018[13]). However, they also change the way jobs are done, requiring workers and companies to adjust, and can make some jobs entirely redundant, putting individuals at risk of displacement. According to OECD estimates, 14% of jobs in countries for which data is available could be automated in the coming 10 to 20 years, and a further 32% of jobs may see significant changes in how they are carried out (Figure 1.5). Finnish jobs face comparatively low risks of being automated or changing significantly in content, yet changes are still likely to affect one in three workers in Finland.

Figure 1.5. Jobs at risk of automation

Share of jobs at high risk of automation or significant change, %

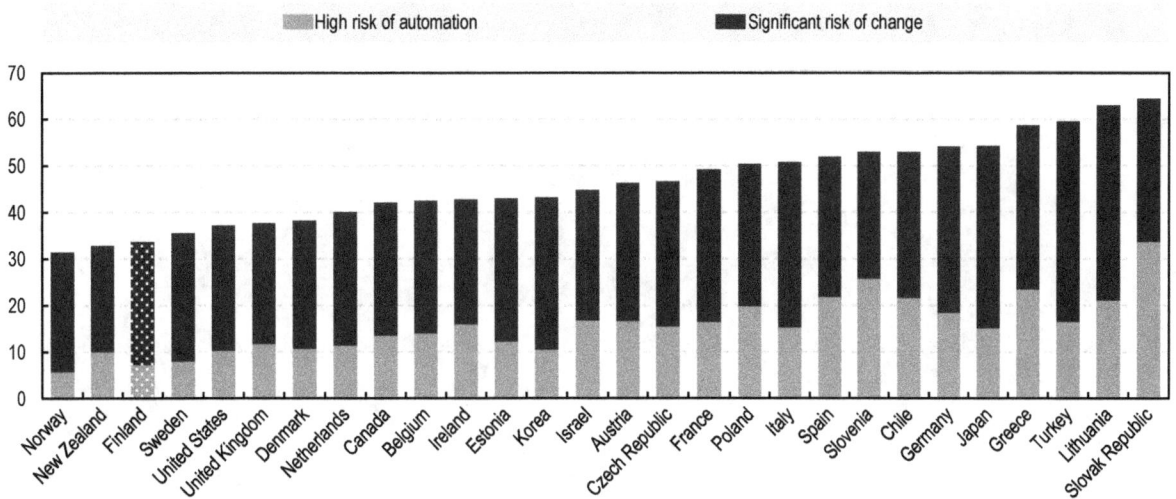

Note: High risk – more than 70% probability of automation; risk of significant change – between 50 and 70% probability. Data for Belgium correspond to Flanders and data for the United Kingdom to England and Northern Ireland.
Source: OECD calculations based on the Survey of Adult Skills (PIAAC) (2012); and Nedelkoska and Quintini (2018[14]), "Automation, skills use and training", https://doi.org/10.1787/2e2f4eea-en.

In this context, the National Forum for Skill Anticipation (*Osaamisen ennakointifoorumi*) finds that more than half of new entrants to the labour force will need higher education degrees to satisfy the skill demands of the future (Finnish National Agency of Education, 2019[15]). It also finds that meta-cognitive skills that enable individuals to analyse and adjust to change, such as problem-solving skills, the ability to learn, and information evaluation skills, will become increasingly important across jobs (Finnish Board of Education, 2019[16]). In terms of more specific skills, skills in customer-related development of services, knowledge of sustainable development, and skills related to digitalisation are highlighted as the most important skills needed for tomorrow's jobs in Finland.

...and population ageing could exacerbate skill shortages in the future.

At the same time, the Finnish working population aged 15-64 is projected to decrease by 57 000 people by 2030 and 208 000 people by 2050 (Figure 1.6). This is equivalent to a 2% and 6% drop in the population, respectively, compared to 2017. Population decline will be unevenly distributed across Finnish regions. It is projected that in 2040, the only region with population growth will be the Uusimaa region due to positive net migration (Statistics Finland, 2019[17]). Populating ageing is expected to lead to skill shortages in the future when, because of both smaller cohorts are replacing retiring workers and changes in labour demand in sectors such as health and care services. Additionally, older workers are playing an increasingly important role in the labour market. Employment rates of 55-64 year olds have risen by close to 30 percentage points in the past 20 years, pointing to a need to keep the skills of workers updated over longer careers.

The extent to which individuals, firms and economies can harness the benefits of these changes in the labour market will critically depend on the ability of the Finnish skill development system to equip people with the right skills. Given the demand for high-level skills in Finland will continue to increase, this will need concerted efforts by public and private actors to shift the entire skill distribution of the adult population upwards towards higher levels.

Figure 1.6. A decreasing working age population

Population by age group 1900-2017 and population projections 2018-70, in millions

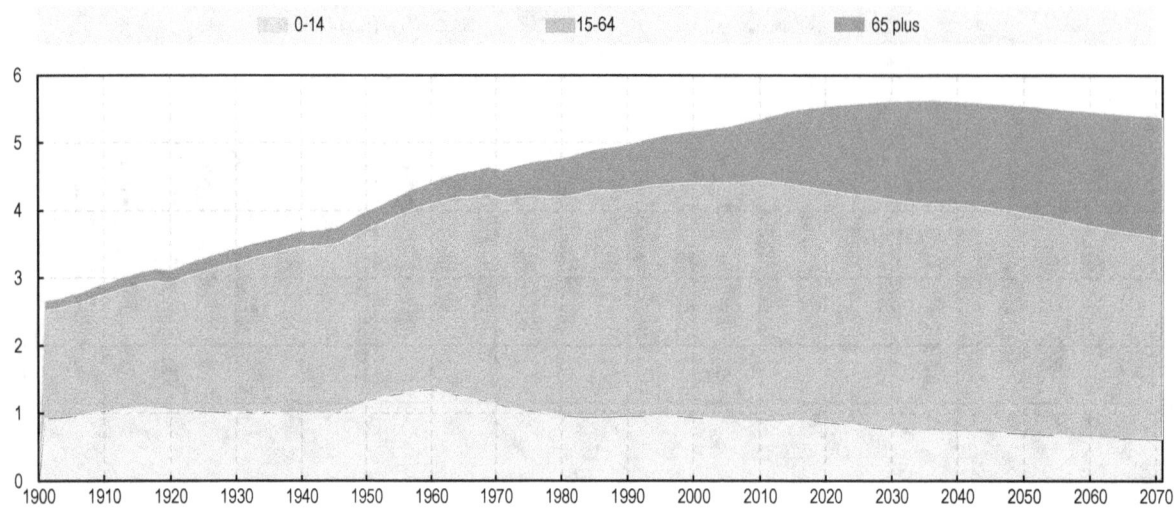

Source: Adapted from Statistics Finland (2018[18]), Population Projection 2018-2070, https://www.stat.fi/til/vaenn/2018/vaenn_2018_2018-11-16_tie_001_en.html.

Skill levels of the adult population

Finland has one of the strongest skill development systems in the world in terms of the proficiency of both young and older people in information processing skills. The country consistently scores amongst the top performing countries in the international skill assessment tests PISA and PIAAC. Large shares of adults aged 25-64 hold tertiary degrees (44%), well above the OECD average (37% in 2017). However, there is some concern that skill and education levels are declining, rather than increasing in line with labour market demand.

The skill levels of the Finnish population are high by international comparison…

According to the 2012 OECD Survey of Adult Skills (PIAAC), Finnish adults display above average literacy and numeracy proficiency, second only to Japan, and above average abilities to solve problems in technology-rich environments (OECD, 2016[19]). The share of adults who do not hold basic information-processing skills is low by international comparison and encompasses around 600 000 people, who have low literacy skills, low numeracy skills, or both (see Chapter 4).

In 2012, 63% of the adult population scored at the three highest proficiency levels in literacy, which is very high in international comparisons but also compared with its Nordic neighbours Norway (55%) and Sweden (58%) (Figure 1.7). The Finnish advantage is slightly smaller when it comes to numeracy, with 58% of the population scoring at the three highest proficiency levels, compared to 57% in Sweden and 55% in Norway. Finnish adults are similarly proficient in technology use than their Nordic neighbours, with 42% scoring at the highest proficiency levels (Norway: 41%, Sweden: 44%). Nevertheless, in Finland, as in all other countries that took part in the OECD Survey of Adult Skills, a substantial proportion of adults have basic or poor problem solving skills in a technology-rich environment.

Figure 1.7. Information-processing skills are some of the highest in the OECD

Adults age 25-64 scoring at proficiency level 3-5 in literacy, numeracy and level 2-3 in problem solving in technology-rich environments, 2012/2015, %

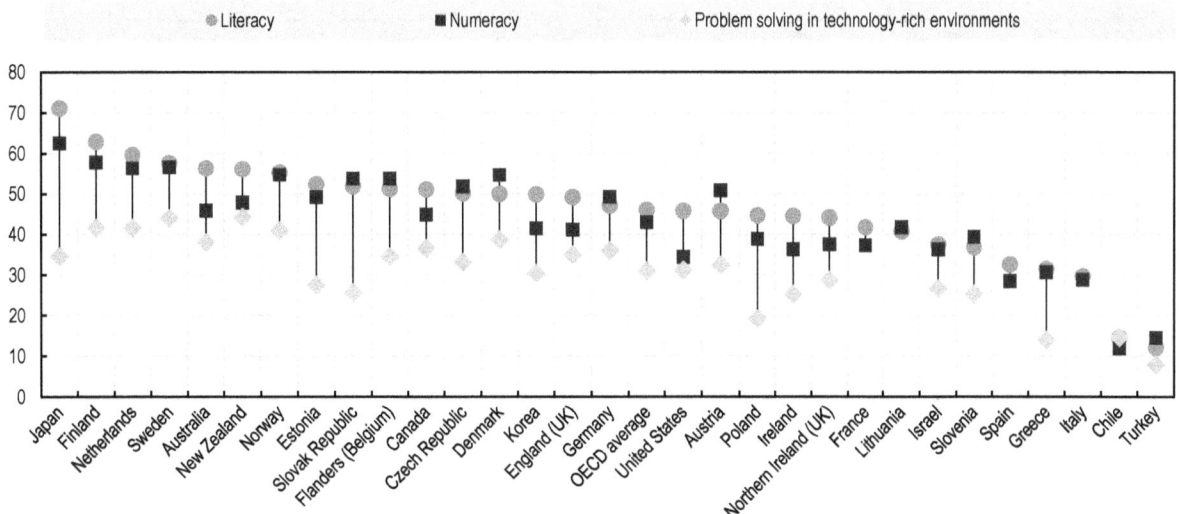

Source: OECD PIAAC data (2012, 2015).

... but there is some concern that skill levels are declining...

Despite these favourable comparisons, there is concern that the skill levels of Finns are declining. Once the top-performing OECD country in PISA, average mathematics, science and reading skills of 15-year olds have declined since 2006, although Finland remains in the group of best performing countries (OECD, 2016[20]). Time-series data on adult skill levels is scant. A comparison of adults' performance in the 2012 PIAAC and the 1998 Adult Literacy Survey (IALS) shows that, while average literacy proficiency increased in this time period for individuals aged 25-65, it decreased for those aged 15-24 (Musset, 2015[21]). This result may be partially explained by later entry of the youngest cohort into tertiary education and a decrease in the years of formal education completed by this point in their lives compared to older cohorts.

In addition, the share of younger Finns obtaining a tertiary degree is declining rather than rising even though the demand for high-level skills has been increasing in the labour market (Figure 1.8). Adults aged 40-44 are now the most educated cohort in history, with 47% holding tertiary degrees. Only 44% of 35-39 year olds and 39% of 30-34 year olds hold tertiary degrees and shares of tertiary attainment in this age group are declining. There is a chance that this gap may close, as adults pursue tertiary degrees later in life, although this cannot be taken for granted given the push to prioritise recent graduates in higher education admission.

Between 31% and 47% of adults in each age group hold tertiary degrees, whether short-cycle tertiary degrees (*opistoaste*) (phased out in the 1990s), bachelor's or master's degrees. This group is well equipped to continue developing their high-level skills over the life-course and often takes up learning opportunities (see below), but may need training offers that are relevant to individual and labour market needs.

Figure 1.8. A decreasing share of younger adults are obtaining tertiary degrees

Share of each age group holding a tertiary degree, percentage, 1970-2017

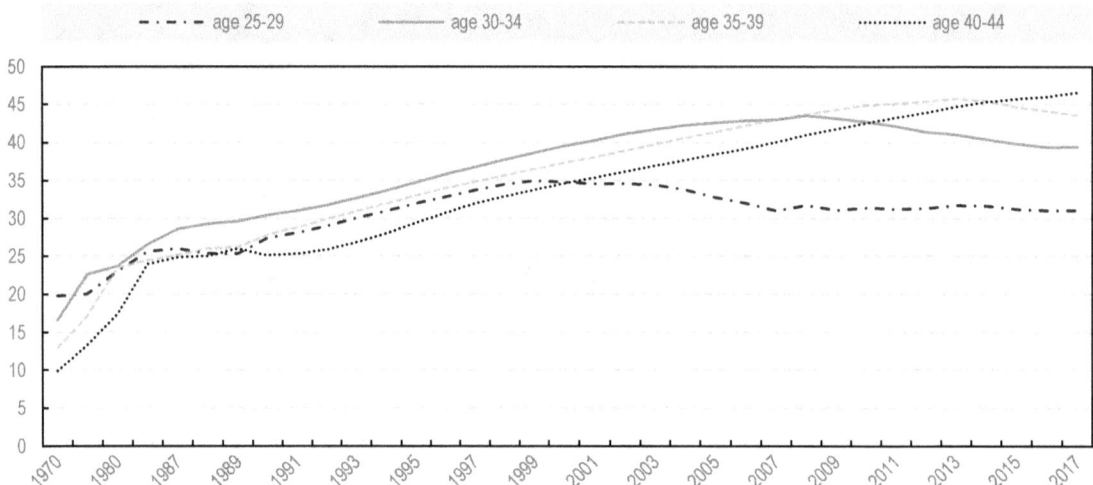

Source: Statistics Finland, Finnish education statistics.

While investment in early-childhood and basic education is essential to equip individuals with strong foundation skills, rapid labour market change suggests that the above described challenges cannot solely be overcome through investment in young people. Today's adults need appropriate opportunities to update and upgrade their skills and acquire new ones on a regular basis throughout their life to improve their labour market prospects and boost the competitiveness of the Finnish economy. Making use of Finland's strong, well-utilised and comprehensively funded adult education system to upskill and reskill the population will be key to aligning skill demand and supply.

Figure 1.9. The group of potential adult learners is diverse

Highest educational attainment by age group, 2017, %

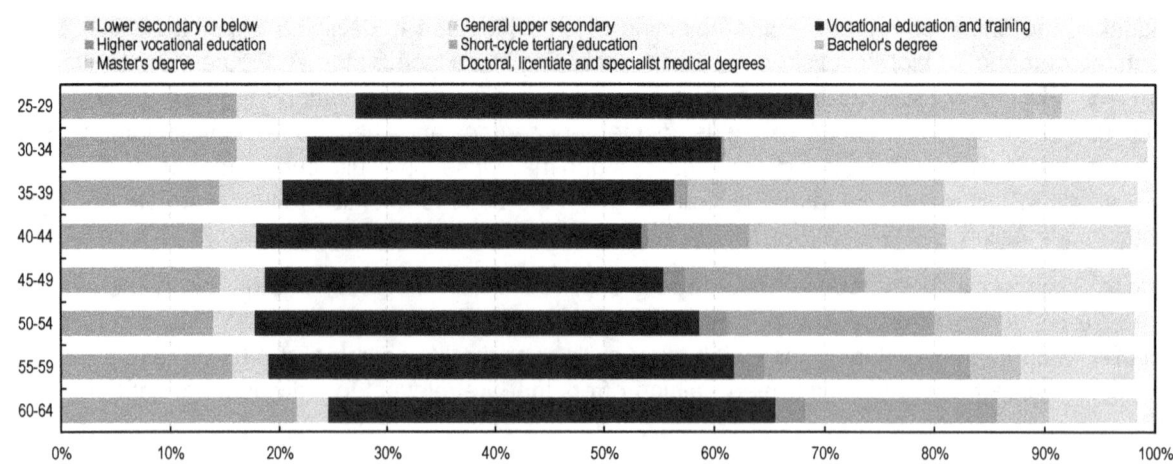

Note: Bachelor's and Master's degrees include degrees at Universities and UAS.
Source: Vipunen education statistics Finland.

Patterns of adult learning participation

International surveys consistently find that Finland has one of the highest participation rates in adult learning in the world. However, participation is likely to be overestimated in comparative data, due to the high shares of people aged 25 and above in Finland who are pursuing initial education and training rather than further training after the completion of initial education. Despite high participation in training, Finland has large participation gaps for some groups, most notably adults with low skills, older workers and the long-term unemployed.

Participation in adult learning is one of the highest in the world…

Just over half of the population aged 25-64 takes part in job-related learning every year (55%), according to OECD PIAAC data. This is the fourth highest adult participation in OECD economies, exceeded only by Denmark (58%), New Zealand (57%) and Norway (56%). However, many adults in Finland face barriers to participating in training. Around 20% of adults would have liked to participate in even more training than they already did and a further 10% would have liked to participate but did not for a variety of reasons. In addition, around 35% of adults did not participate in job-related learning and did not want to for various reasons, including a lack of motivation or awareness of the potential benefits from engaging in training.

Figure 1.10. More than half of Finnish adults participate in job-related learning

Adults aged 25-64 who participated in job-related education and training in the past 12 months, 2012/2015, %

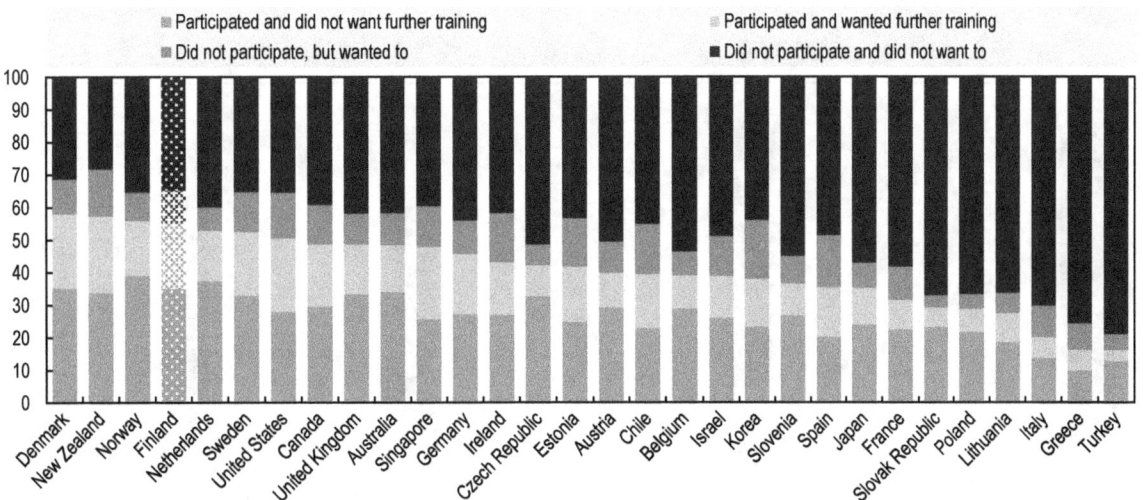

Note: Formal and non-formal job-related education and training.
Source: OECD PIAAC data (2012, 2015).

While adult learning participation in Finland is high by international standards, there has been some concern about decreasing participation rates. These concerns are primarily driven by results of the 2016 Adult Education Survey (AES), which recorded a drop of 3.2 percentage points compared to the previous wave in 2011 (see also Ruuskanen and Niemi (2018[22])). However, this drop may be due to changes in the mode of data collection (see evidence from Sweden facing similar issues: (Statistics Sweden, 2017[23])). Analysis of European Labour Force survey data (LFS) shows opposite trends, with adult participation in education and training steadily increasing since 2009 and sharper yearly increases since 2016 (Figure 1.11). This poses the question of which data source best reflects the true picture of trends in training participation.

There are a number of possible explanations for the discrepancies between the two sources, including differences in the coverage period (4-week vs. 12-month window), differences in the structure of the surveys (general labour market vs. life-long learning survey) and differences in the definition of learning activities (Goglio and Meroni, 2014[24]). In the case of Finland, an additional difference between AES and LFS arises from the fact that the AES data published by the Finnish statistical office only refers to participation in specific educational programmes that are traditionally considered adult learning.[2] The discrepancy between AES and LFS may therefore reflect a decrease in adult participation in these traditional forms of adult learning, but an increase in participation in other education and training opportunities, for example initial vocational degrees or regular degree education at universities and universities of applied sciences (UAS). Data by the Finnish statistical office indeed confirms an increased participation of older adults in initial vocational education and training, as well as degree courses at UAS and to a lesser degree universities (see Chapter 3).

An additional explanation for the discrepancy lies in the different reference periods for both data sources. As the LFS measures the share of adults participating in a 4-week time period, it effectively measures 'training events' rather than 'participants' in a given year. An increase in the LFS may reflect the same individuals participating more often over the year or for longer time-periods, not necessarily an increase in the learning population (Goglio and Meroni, 2014[24]). There is no data available that could confirm this suggested increase in repeated participation by individuals.

Figure 1.11. Time trends of participation provide a mixed-picture depending on data source

Adults age 25-64 who participated in education and training in the past 4 weeks (LFS) and 12 months (AES), %

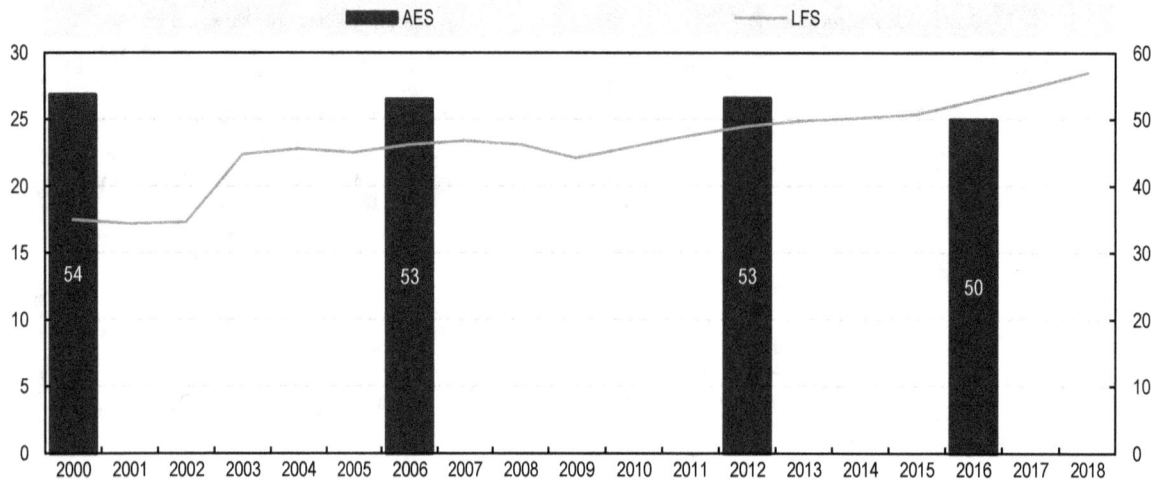

Note: For AES definition of adult education and training as per Ruuskanen and Niemi (2018[22]), Osallistuminen Aikuiskoulutukseen. Vuonna 2017 [Participation in Adult Education. In 2017]; for LFS definition includes all formal and non-formal learning, break in time series 2003.
Source: Statistics Finland (AES 2006, 2012, 2016, national adult education survey 2000); Eurostat (LFS, yearly averages).

Adult learners in Finland participate in 156 hours of non-formal learning on average, which is equivalent to just under four weeks of full-time study per year (Figure 1.12). Learning intensity is high by international comparison, only in Denmark (167 hours) and Slovenia (180 hours) do adult learners spend more time learning. Other Nordic neighbours display much lower intensity: Adult learners in Norway, for example, receive around half the instruction time. This can likely be explained by the pervasiveness of longer course options in Finland's adult learning provision (see Chapter 3).

Figure 1.12. Learning intensity in Finland is high

Mean hours of instruction received by participants in non-formal learning activities, age 25-64, 2016

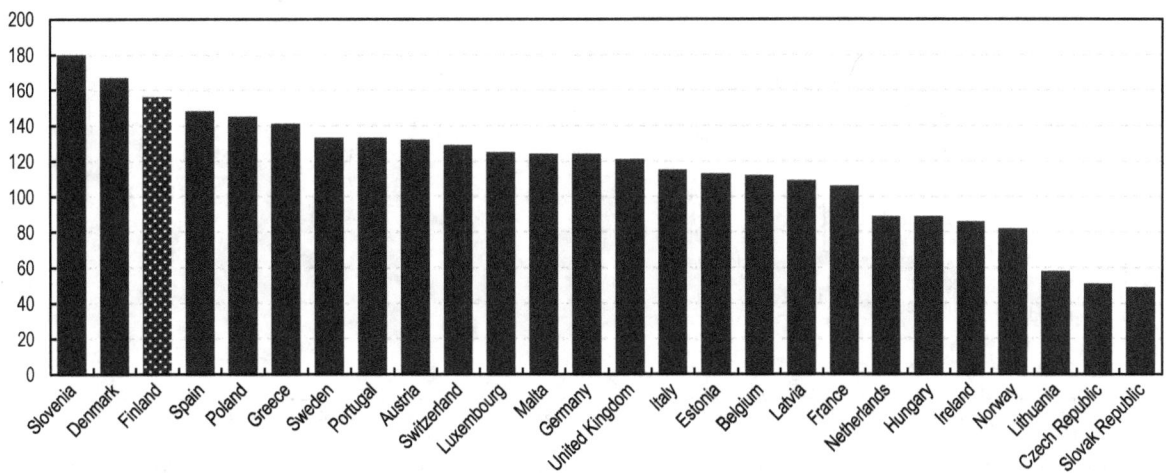

Note: Refers only to participation in non-formal learning.
Source: Eurostat, AES data (2016).

...but some groups are at risk of being left behind.

Not everyone in Finland takes part in adult learning to the same extent and some of the groups who would strongly benefit are the least likely to participate. According to PIAAC data, 29% of all low-skilled adults participate in job-related learning, while 60% of those with medium to high-skills do. Participation gaps between prime age and older adults (64% vs. 35%), the employed and long-term unemployed (66% vs. 33%) and workers in jobs at high and low risk of automation are similarly large (53% vs. 74%) Figure 1.13).This is problematic for a number of reasons, including that it implies that continuous learning widens the skill gap between advantaged and less advantaged adults.

According to the OECD's ranking of the performance of each country's adult learning systems, Finland has one of the least inclusive systems across the OECD, exceeded only by Chile, Germany, the Netherlands and the Slovak Republic (OECD, 2019[25]). Finland has the largest participation gaps of all OECD economies when it comes to adults with low skill levels or low wages relative to those with, respectively, higher skills or higher wages. For individuals, firms and economies to respond to changes in the labour market, it is imperative for Finland to find ways to make its adult learning system more inclusive (see Chapter 4).

The role of formal adult education is increasing...

As in most countries, the bulk of learning takes place informally in Finland, with 69% of adults taking part in non-institutionalised learning activities every year, e.g. learning from peers, according to AES data. Close to one in two adults take part in non-formal learning (48%), i.e. in courses of short duration and/or not leading to a certification, while a smaller share of adults takes part in formal learning (14%). Participation in formal and informal learning has increased in Finland over the past decade, while non-formal learning participation has decreased. This is the inverse of the pattern for the EU28 as whole, where there was an increase in informal and non-formal learning, as well as a slight decrease of formal learning (Figure 1.14).

Figure 1.13. There are large participation gaps between groups

Adults age 25-64 who participated in education and training, by group, 2012, %

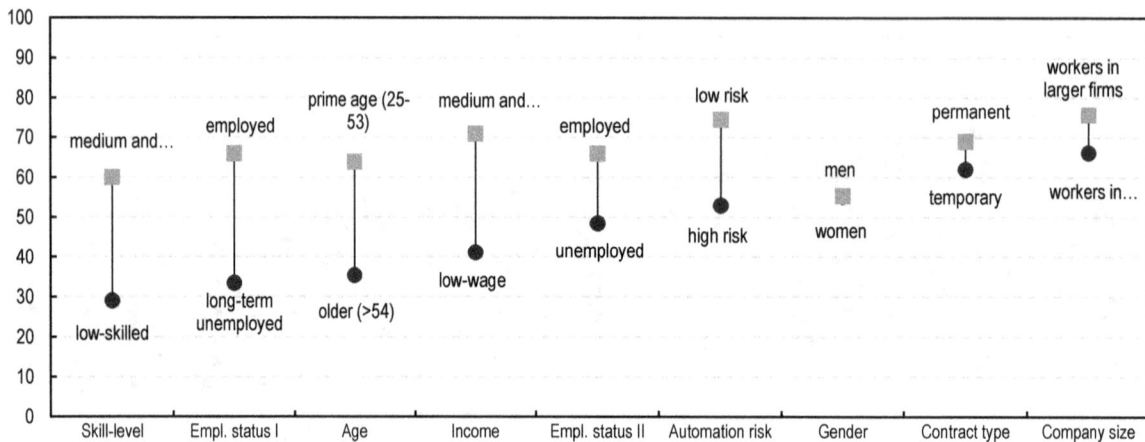

Note: The baseline varies across categories, e.g. skill-level refers to all adults, while contract type refers to employed adults only. Low-skilled refers to adults scoring at level 1 or below in literacy and/or numeracy in PIAAC; long-term unemployed are defined at those who have been unemployed for 12 months or more; low-wage refers to workers who earn at most two third of the national median wage; high risk of automation refers to adults in jobs with at least 70% probability of automation; temporary refers to workers in temporary contracts; workers in SMEs refers to workers in enterprises between 1 and 249 employees.
Source: OECD PIAAC data (2012).

By age, the increase in formal learning in Finland was strongest for the younger age groups. Participation by 25-34 year olds increased from 24% to 32% between 2007 and 2016. A smaller increase from 11% to 15% was observed for those aged 35-44. This raises the question of whether the observed increase in formal adult learning participation is in reality a symptom of increasingly drawn-out initial education careers.

It should also be noted that it is becoming difficult to distinguish between formal and non-formal learning in Finland. Modularisation, the possibility to take partial degrees and recognition of prior learning have blurred the lines between the two forms of learning. Non-formal learning is becoming increasingly formalised.

Figure 1.14. Inverse trends in Finland and the EU-28 in the importance of different forms of training

Adults age 25-64 who participated in formal, non-formal and informal learning, %

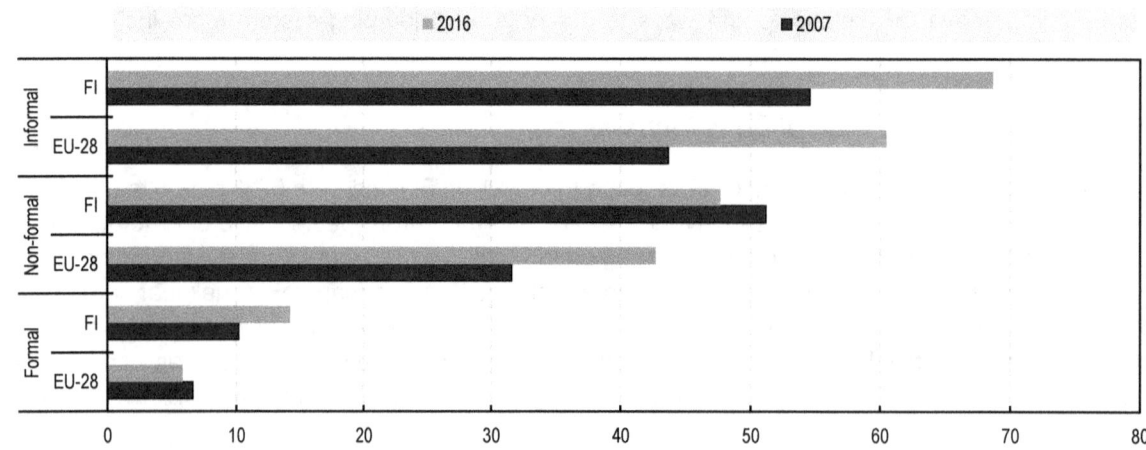

Source: Eurostat, AES data (2016).

..., but the available data may overestimate participation.

As defined in this report, adult learners are individuals who have finalised their initial education including higher education and are re-entering the education system to upskill or reskill, typically after having spent time in the labour market. However, this definition is not reflected in the data presented above. Official published statistics from international surveys (AES, LFS and PIAAC) count all adults aged 25 and over in education as adult learners, irrespective of whether this learning constitutes part of their initial degree.

Young people in Finland often have longer initial education careers than in other countries. In particular, they start later and take longer to complete higher education. The average age of graduation with a Bachelors' degree is 28 years, significantly higher than the OECD average of 26 years. Master's graduates are on average 32 years of age, compared to an OECD average of 30 years. This is likely to overestimate adult learning participation in Finland compared to other countries. An exact assessment of the extent of the issue is difficult. However, it can be shown that the group of 25-34 year olds in formal education make up a high share of 'adult learners' (Figure 1.15). One can assume that a significant share of this group represents young adults still completing their initial education.

Figure 1.15. A high share of adult learners are young adults in formal education

25-34 year olds in formal education as share of total adult learners, 2016, %

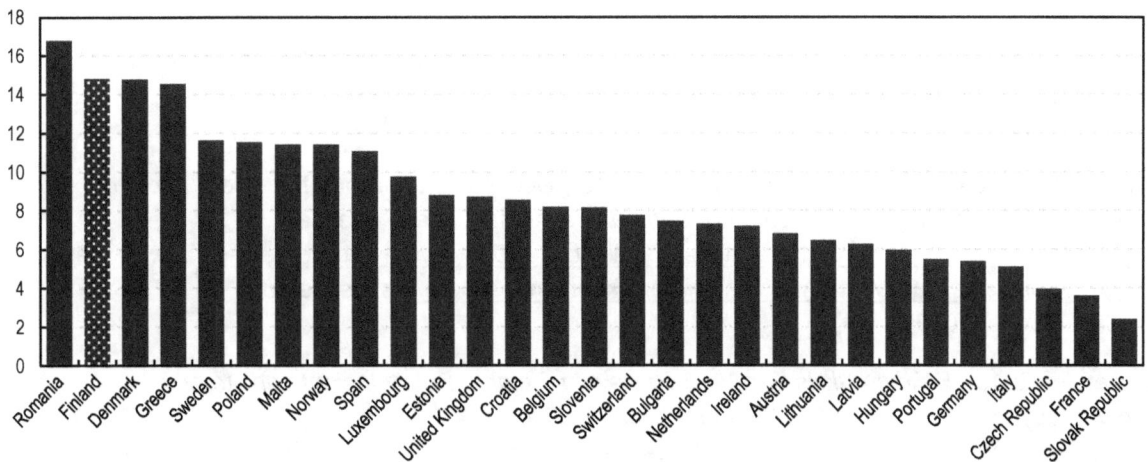

Source: OECD elaboration based on Eurostat, AES and population statistics.

References

Eurostat (2016), *Classification of learning activities (CLA) manual : 2016 edition.*, Publications Office of the European Union, Luxembourg. [1]

Finnish Board of Education (2019), *Osaaminen 2035 - Osaamisen ennakointifoorumin ensimmäisiä ennakointituloksia [Expertise 2035 - First Foresight Results from the Foresight Forum]*, Finnish Board of Education, Helsinki, http://www.oph.fi. [16]

Finnish Government (2019), *Inclusive and competent Finland - a socially, economically and ecologically sustainable society*, Publication of the Finnish Government, Helsinki, http://julkaisut.valtioneuvosto.fi/bitstream/handle/10024/161664/Inclusive%20and%20competent%20Finland_2019.pdf?sequence=7&isAllowed=y (accessed on 8 July 2019). [7]

Finnish National Agency of Education (2019), *Work life changes - how does education respond? Proposals published by the Knowledge Forecasting Forum Board of Education*, https://www.oph.fi/fi/uutiset/2019/tyoelama-muuttuu-miten-koulutus-vastaa-osaamisen-ennakointifoorumi-julkisti (accessed on 9 August 2019). [15]

Goglio, V. and E. Meroni (2014), *Adult participation in lifelong learning. The impact of using a 12-months or 4-weeks reference period*, Joint Research Center of the European Commission, http://dx.doi.org/10.2788/43117. [24]

Ministry of Economic Affairs and Employment (2019), *Occupational barometer: Labour shortage in many occupations*, https://tem.fi/en/article/-/asset_publisher/ammattibarometri-tyovoimapula-vaivaa-yha-useampaa-ammattia (accessed on 9 July 2019). [10]

Ministry of Economic Affairs and Employment (2019), *Occupational barometer: The number of occupations suffering from labour shortage has decreased*, Press release, https://valtioneuvosto.fi/en/article/-/asset_publisher/1410877/ammattibarometri-tyovoimapulasta-karsivien-ammattien-maara-kaantynyt-laskuun (accessed on 18 December 2019). [11]

Musset, P. (2015), *Building Skills For All: A Review of Finland. Policy Insights on literacy, numeracy and digital skills from the survey of adult skills*, OECD, Paris, http://www.oecd.org/finland/Building-Skills-For-All-A-Review-of-Finland.pdf (accessed on 19 April 2019). [21]

Nedelkoska, L. and G. Quintini (2018), "Automation, skills use and training", *OECD Social, Employment and Migration Working Papers*, No. 202, OECD Publishing, Paris, https://dx.doi.org/10.1787/2e2f4eea-en. [14]

OECD (2019), *Getting Skills Right: Future-Ready Adult Learning Systems*, Getting Skills Right, OECD Publishing, Paris, https://dx.doi.org/10.1787/9789264311756-en. [25]

OECD (2019), *Investing in Youth: Finland*, OECD Publishing, Paris, https://doi.org/10.1787/1251a123-en. [8]

OECD (2019), *OECD Economic Outlook, Volume 2019 Issue 1*, OECD Publishing, Paris, https://dx.doi.org/10.1787/b2e897b0-en. [6]

OECD (2018), *OECD Economic Surveys: Finland 2018*, OECD Publishing, Paris, https://doi.org/10.1787/eco_surveys-fin-2018-en. [2]

OECD (2018), *Putting faces to the jobs at risk of automation*, OECD, Paris, http://www.oecd.org/employment/future-of-work.htm (accessed on 21 August 2019). [13]

OECD (2018), *Skills for jobs*, OECD, Paris, http://www.oecdskillsforjobsdatabase.org (accessed on 18 April 2019). [12]

OECD (2017), *OECD Employment Outlook 2017*, OECD Publishing, Paris, https://dx.doi.org/10.1787/empl_outlook-2017-en. [9]

OECD (2016), *OECD Economic Surveys: Finland 2016*, OECD Publishing, Paris, https://doi.org/10.1787/eco_surveys-fin-2016-en (accessed on 5 March 2019). [3]

OECD (2016), *PISA 2015 Results (Volume I): Excellence and Equity in Education*, PISA, OECD Publishing, Paris, https://dx.doi.org/10.1787/9789264266490-en. [20]

OECD (2016), *Skills Matter: Further Results from the Survey of Adult Skills*, OECD Skills Studies, OECD Publishing, Paris, https://dx.doi.org/10.1787/9789264258051-en. [19]

OECD (2014), *OECD Economic Surveys: Finland 2014*, OECD Publishing, Paris, https://doi.org/10.1787/eco_surveys-fin-2014-en (accessed on 8 July 2019). [4]

OECD (2012), *OECD Economic Surveys: Finland 2012*, OECD Publishing, Paris, https://dx.doi.org/10.1787/eco_surveys-fin-2012-en. [5]

Ruuskanen, T. and H. Niemi (2018), *Osallistuminen Aikuiskoulutukseen. Vuonna 2017 [Participation in Adult Education. In 2017]*, Statistics Finland, Helsinki, http://www.stat.fi (accessed on 23 July 2019). [22]

Statistics Finland (2019), *The decline in the birth rate is reflected in the population development of areas*, https://www.stat.fi/til/vaenn/2019/vaenn_2019_2019-09-30_tie_001_en.html (accessed on 18 December 2019). [17]

Statistics Finland (2018), *Population projection 2018-2070*, Statistics Finland, Helsinki, https://www.stat.fi/til/vaenn/2018/vaenn_2018_2018-11-16_en.pdf (accessed on 18 April 2019). [18]

Statistics Sweden (2017), *Break in time series AES2016*, Statistics Sweden. [23]

Notes

[1] Source: Statistics Finland, Labour Force Survey data, indicator: 11pw, own calculations.

[2] Institutions include: adult and evening secondary education, apprenticeships, vocational training institutes, polytechnics and adult education centres, open polytechnics, continuous vocational training courses at universities or colleges and their continuing education centres, training activities for summer universities, non-vocational training of folk high schools, non-vocational training of music schools, sports colleges, training provided by civic and labour colleges, training in language schools, training provided by organisations, study clubs, dance schools, course training organised by the employer, training activities of specific training firms of training centres, conferences, seminars and similar training events, other education and training and studying abroad.

2 The continuous learning system

To assess the readiness of the Finnish continuous learning system to respond to ongoing changes in the labour market, it is essential to understand the key features of the system. Therefore, this chapter sketches out the basic features of the current system, how it is governed and financed. It also provides a brief overview of the structure of adult learning provision. Finland has a long history of adult learning and a highly developed continuous learning system. Adults can access a wide range of learning opportunities at all skill levels. There is little distinction between youth and adult learners and both groups typically learn alongside each other. Public or quasi-public actors play a strong role in the regulation, funding and delivery of continuous learning.

Introduction

Along with other countries, Finland needs to strengthen the responsiveness of its continuous learning system to the ongoing changes in the labour market brought about by the megatrends of population ageing, technological change and globalisation.

It benefits from a long tradition of adult education, the origins of which reach back to the 19th century, and an adult learning system that has successfully adapted to changing demands over time. In the 1990s, for example, adult education was subject to major reforms, driven by the need to modernise the system and the introduction of a more market-oriented approach to education (OECD, 2001[1]). Various acts setting out the legal framework for adult education stem from this time. Further large reforms were implemented in 2009 in the context of the global economic and financial crisis, which expanded education services and aimed to improve the focus on disadvantaged groups (Desjardins, 2017[27]).

After some years of more limited attention to the topic, Finnish governments have recently refocused on continuous learning in the context of the challenges outlined in Chapter 1. The 2019 government programme, for example, makes frequent mention of the topic and has announced a comprehensive parliamentary reform of continuous learning to be developed in tripartite cooperation (Finnish Government, 2019[7]).

This chapter provides key background information on the current governance, financing and structure of adult learning provision in Finland. It aims to contextualise the main challenges regarding future-ready and inclusive adult learning provision that are subsequently identified in Chapters 3 and 4.

Governance

The responsibility for continuous learning is shared within and across ministries...

As in many countries, the responsibility for the development of a continuous learning policy is shared within and across government ministries. Most of the continuous learning system is under the responsibility of the Ministry of Education and Culture (MoEC) and spread across different departments. The *Department for General Upper Secondary Education and Vocational Education and Training* is responsible for adult general and vocational education. The *Department for Higher Education and Science Policy* is responsible for adult higher education. Finally, the *Department for Early Childhood Education, Comprehensive School Education and Liberal Adult Education* covers adult liberal education. The responsibilities of the Ministry of Economic Affairs and Employment (MoEE) include vocational labour market training (not leading to a qualification) and integration training.

Coordination between ministries primarily takes place in the form of working groups, set up by either Ministry. For example, in 2019, a working group on developing continuous learning developed a description of the models and principles for continuous learning and proposed key levers for further development (Ministry of Education and Culture, 2019[28]). The group included members of the MoEC and MoEE, the Ministry of Finance, the Ministry of Social Affairs and Health, alongside social partner and civil society organisations. At the political level, coordination takes places through the Employment, Education and Economic Affairs Council, which is composed of members of the MoEC, MoEE, Ministry of Interior (MoI), Ministry of Social Affairs and Health (MoSAH), Ministry of Finance (MoF) and the Social Partners.

A number of other agencies and expert bodies support the work of the MoEC. The Finnish National Agency for Education (*Opetushallitus/ Utbildningsstyrelsen*) assists the Ministry by developing education and training, including through educational standards, core curricula and qualification requirements. It also hosts the National Skill Anticipation Forum (*Osaamisen ennakointifoorumi*) for the anticipation of skill needs. Evaluating the operations of education providers is the responsibility of the Finnish Education Evaluation Centre (*Kansallinen koulutuksen arviointikeskus/ Nationella centret för utbildningsutvärdering*).

Implementing agencies of the MoEE are the Centres for Economic Development, Transport and the Environment (*elinkeino-, liikenne ja ympäristökeskus, ELY centres/ Närings-, trafik- och miljöcentralen, NTM-centralerna*), which themselves supervise the activities of the Employment and Economic Development offices (*TE-toimisto/ TE-palvelut*), the Finnish public employment services.

...as well as with municipalities and learning providers

At the regional level, 311 municipalities have substantial responsibilities for skill development policy, covering early childhood education and care, basic and general upper secondary education, and Adult Liberal Education. Their responsibilities encompass funding allocation, staff recruitment, as well as curriculum design and implementation.

Education and training providers have a high degree of autonomy in the Finnish education system (Desjardins, 2017[27]). Continuous learning providers are predominately public or quasi-public education institutions. There is only a very limited presence of private education and training companies. Where they exist, they typically serve employers for the purpose of staff training (e.g. ICT or languages), rather than individuals themselves. One of the reasons for this is that most adult education is provided free of charge or at a very low cost to the individual (see below). This makes it more challenging for private providers to break into the market.

Non-state actors have a limited role in the Finnish adult learning system. Social partners and civil society organisations, such as the Finnish Adult Education Association, typically have a consultative role in the policy-making process. For example, a number of social partner organisations have recently been involved in the aforementioned working group on developing continuous learning.

The current system lacks an overarching strategy

At the point of writing, Finland lacks an overarching strategy on the development of continuous learning, which brings together the work of these different actors. While Finland has a tradition of five-year Education and Research Development Plans, no such plan was in place between 2012 and 2019 (Ministry of Education and Culture, 2008[29]; Ministry of Education and Culture, 2012[30]). These plans used to be a key reference document for Finnish education and research policy, including concrete actions and targets for the implementation of the government programme.

The current government is reconnecting with this tradition and is in the process of developing an education policy report, which is due to be submitted to parliament by the end of 2020. Additionally, it is in the process of developing a comprehensive strategy on continuous learning in working life through a parliamentary reform process, which involves all parliamentary parties, social partners and education providers (Finnish Government, 2019[7]).

Financing

Direct costs of participation are low for individuals...

Given the dispersed responsibilities for adult learning, it has traditionally been difficult to assess the total amount of funding available for adult learning in Finland. In 2018, the Finnish innovation fund SITRA published a full costing exercise of the Finnish life-long learning system. It estimated that EUR 18.9 billion (8.4% of GDP) was spent on life-long learning from early childhood to adult education in 2017 (Aho and Ranki, 2018[31]). According to the authors, approximately one quarter of this amount represented spending on adult education, which excluded the costs of adults learning in the formal initial education system. This may be an underestimate, given that adults also take part in the regular education system such as vocational or higher education (see below).

The direct costs of education and training, i.e. the costs of running a programme are shared between employers, individuals and the government:

- A large share of the cost is borne by **private employers**, who pay EUR 1-1.5 billion per year for training costs depending on the estimate (Aho and Ranki, 2018[31]; Kauhanen, 2018[32]). In addition, **public employers** pay around EUR 174 million on training.
- It is estimated that **individuals** pay around EUR 500 million for course-related costs in upper secondary, vocational and adult education, such as for materials and tools and – in the case of some types of adult education – enrolment and participation fees. It is important to note, that some of these costs relate to those in initial education and that these numbers are rough estimates, which should be treated with caution (Aho and Ranki, 2018[31]).
- **Government** spending in the sub-sectors most often used by adults (vocational, higher and liberal adult education, as well as labour market training) was estimated to be just under EUR 5 billion per year. As adults over the age of 25 constitute more than half of all learners in these sub-sectors, it can be assumed that government spending on adult education and training is at least EUR 2.5 billion per year.

Figure 2.1. Government is key funder of adult learning

Estimated funding for adult learning provision, 2017

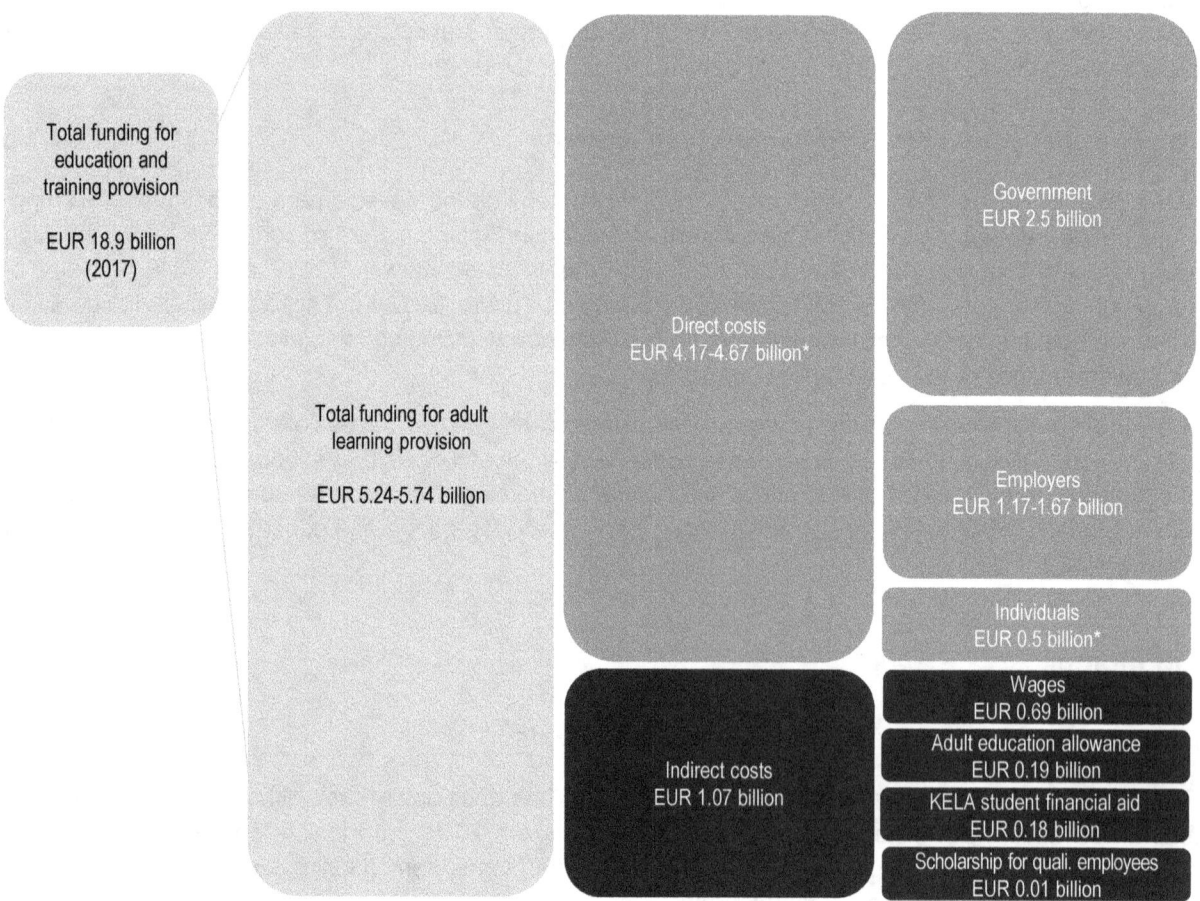

Note: All data are estimates, *includes funds relating to initial education.
Source: OECD estimates based on Aho and Ranki (2018[31]), *Milla Rahalla?*, Sitra, Helsinki and Kauhanen (2018[32]), *Yksilön, yrityksen ja yhteiskunnan vastuu työuranaikaisessa kouluttautumisessa*, No 67, ETLA Muistio, Helsinki, https://pub.etla.fi/ETLA-Muistio-Brief-67.pdf.

...and a wide range of financial support is available

Living costs of adults in education and training, i.e. indirect costs of learning, are either covered by employers through the continued payment of wages or through allowances and study support. The funding to support living costs amounts to approximately EUR 1 billion per year (Aho and Ranki, 2018[31]; Employment Fund, 2019[33]; Kela, 2019[34]):

- **Wages**: When adults take part in training organised by their employer, they typically continue to receive their regular salaries. SITRA estimates that employers pay around EUR 691 million in wages during training participation. This amount is composed of EUR 34 million paid to public sector staff in central government, EUR 157 million paid to public sector staff in municipalities and an estimated EUR 500 million paid by private employers.
- **Adult Education Allowance**: Adults who take up un-paid educational leave of 2 to 15 months, have an employment history of at least 8 years and an income of EUR 250 per month or less are eligible for support through the Adult Education Allowance. The allowance has a basic and an income related component. The minimum amount paid is EUR 592.11 per month, yet on average individuals receive EUR 1 460 per month. The amount received is subject to tax. In 2017, the Employment Fund paid EUR 188 million in Adult Education Allowance. While the full allowance is reserved for full-time study, adults can access an Adjusted Adult Education Allowance for part-time study. A reform of the Adult Education Allowance is ongoing, which aims to increase flexibility and take-up amongst disadvantaged groups. Legal changes are expected to come into effect in 2020.
- **Scholarship for qualified employees**: Employees with at least 5 years of employment history can receive a EUR 400 scholarship upon completion of a vocational upper secondary qualification, a further qualification or a specialist qualification. In 2017, the Employment Fund paid EUR 9.9 million for these scholarships.
- **Financial aid for students**: Individuals can receive financial aid from the Finnish Social Insurance Institution KELA to participate in formal education below the lower secondary level (including adult basic education). Individuals are eligible for a study grant, a government-guaranteed student loan and a housing allowance (under some circumstances). These benefits are paid in addition to other benefits received. Individuals receive an average of EUR 385 per month. In 2017, a total of EUR 606.6 million was paid. As 29% of individuals receiving aid are aged 25 or above, it can be estimated that adult learners received about EUR 175.914 million from KELA.
- **Social Assistance** for unemployed in training amounts to EUR 91 million per year (2016).

Yet, investment may be lagging behind the other Nordic countries

While the SITRA report provides a good overview of the funding situation in Finland, internationally comparable data on the financing of adult learning is extremely limited, making it difficult to benchmark Finnish investment against other countries. The most relevant data are about one decade old (FiBS/DIE, 2013[35]), are based on rough estimates, and should be treated as indicative of actual spending levels at best. It shows that, amongst the countries analysed, spending levels on adult learning are the highest in the Nordic countries, which spend between 1.7 and 2.2% of GDP on adult learning (Figure 2.2). This is about 20% of all spending on education in these countries (FiBS/DIE, 2013[35]). Among the Nordic countries, Finland was estimated as having somewhat lower investment in adult learning, with the smallest contribution of individuals to the financing and a stronger involvement of the PES.

Figure 2.2. Investment in adult learning is high by international comparison

Expenditures for adult learning as a % of GDP, persons ages 25 and over, 2009

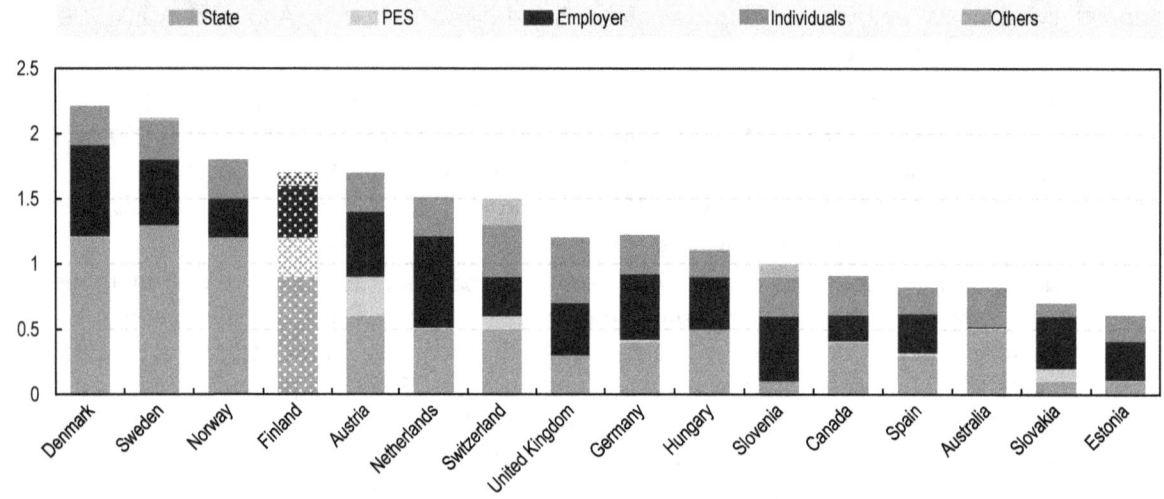

Note: Data includes spending on higher education for adults aged 25 years and older; without private spending on higher education; no data on higher education for SVN; different reference years for CAN (2008), CHE (2007), DEU (2008/2010), GBR (2008), NDL (2010), SVN (2011).
Source: FiBS/DIE (2013[35]), Developing the Adult Learning Sector. Annex to the final report, http://lll.mon.bg/uploaded_files/financingannex_en.pdf.

Data on investment in specific sub-sectors of the adult learning system are easier to obtain (Figure 2.3). Evidence from the OECD Labour Market Policy database suggests that Finland strongly invests in training via active labour market policies with 0.44% of GDP spent on training-related ALMPs in 2017, only surpassed by Denmark (0.52%) in the OECD area. Norway and Sweden record much lower investment through these channels, around the OECD average 0.12%.

Figure 2.3. Public investment is high, while company investment is lagging behind

Share of GDP invested in training-related ALMPs (2017) and share of training of all company investments (2017), %

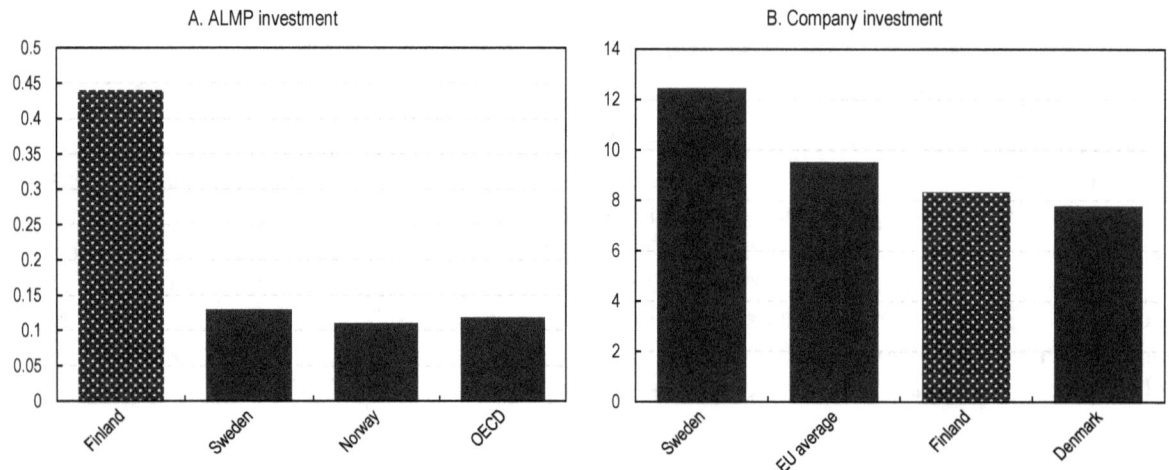

Note: Company investment in training expressed as share of total investment made.
Source: A. OECD LMP database, B. EIB Investment survey.

As described above, employers bear much of the cost of adult learning in Finland. However, by international standards, investment of employers lags behind. Data from the Continuing Vocational Training Survey (CVTS) highlight that the vast majority of Finnish companies (83%) with more than 10 employees fully or partly finance education and training measures of their employees. This share is slightly lower than in other Nordic countries (DNK: 87%, NOR: 99%, SWE: 93%). Evidence from the EIB Investment Survey also shows that the relative share of investment by companies in training is below EU average. While around 8% of all firm investments in Finland are in training, this share is 9% across the EU and highest in Luxembourg (22%), France (14%), Portugal and Sweden (both 13%) (Figure 2.3). Together, this evidence suggests that companies in Finland may be taking on a smaller share of the overall burden of spending on adult training than in some other countries.

Structure of provision

This section provides a brief overview of the adult learning system in Finland. Further detailed information about different kinds of learning provision can be found in Chapter 3.

Adults and young people learn alongside each other…

The Finnish adult learning system encompasses a wide range of formal and non-formal learning opportunities at different levels, including basic and general education, vocational education, higher education, adult liberal education and staff training (employee training organised by employers). With the exception of basic and general education, there is little distinction between adult and youth education and both groups learn alongside each other at the same educational institutions. Table 2.1 provides an overview of the range of formal and non-formal adult learning provision available in Finland (see Chapter 3 for further detail).

It should be noted that there is some degree of overlap between different types of provision. Staff training, for example, makes use of other public provision, namely formal and non-formal vocational training and in-service training provided by higher education institutions.

Table 2.1. Types of formal and non-formal adult learning provision in Finland

Basic and general education	Vocational education	Higher education	Adult liberal education	Staff training
Basic education qualification Basic education subject studies General upper secondary qualification General upper secondary generation subject studies	Initial vocational qualification Further vocational qualifications Specialist vocational qualifications Non-formal VET/ short courses Labour market training	Bachelor's degree Master's degree Open Studies Professional specialisation studies In-service training	Non-formal learning activities	Courses commissioned by employers Joint-purchase training

Source: Own elaboration, basic outline following Desjardins (2017[27]).

…and learning typically takes place in public or government-dependent education institutions

The vast majority of adult learning provision in Finland is delivered by public education institutions or government-dependent private institutions, such as specialised vocational institutions owned by enterprises. Independent private education providers play a limited role. Table 2.2 below summarises the type of education providers involved in the delivery of formal and non-formal learning opportunities in Finland.

Table 2.2. Types of education providers involved in the delivery of adult learning in Finland

Basic and general education	Vocational education	Higher education	Adult liberal education	Staff training
Upper secondary schools for adults General upper secondary schools Vocational schools Folk high schools Adult education centres	Vocational institutions *For labour market training also:* Universities Universities of Applied Sciences Adult Education Centres Folk High Schools Private providers	Universities Universities of Applied Sciences	Adult Education Centres Folk High Schools Summer universities Study centres Vocational institutions	Vocational schools Universities Universities of Applied Sciences Adult Education Centres Folk High Schools Summer universities Study centres Private providers

Source: Own elaboration, basic outline following Desjardins (2017[27]).

The distinction between formal and non-formal learning opportunities can be blurred

It can be difficult to distinguish between formal and non-formal learning opportunities in the Finnish context, as non-formal learning opportunities constitute the building blocks for gaining a formal qualification. Adults taking (non-formal) learning modules as open university studies, for example, can get them recognised towards a formal qualification when they register as degree students. Different from open university systems in many other OECD countries, Open University Studies in Finland are run by individual higher education institutions. Typically, Open University Studies encompass the same courses and modules that are also offered through degree studies at Universities and UAS.

For the same reason, lines between job-related and liberal education are blurred. Participation in Open University courses may be considered Adult Liberal Education, or popular education, when taken for recreational purposes. Given the role of Open University credentials in obtaining formal higher qualifications in Finland, they are here considered part of the higher education system.

References

Aho, M. and S. Ranki (2018), *Milla Rahalla?*, Sitra, Helsinki, http://www.sitra.fi. [7]

Employment Fund (2019), *Benefits for adult students*, Employment Fund webpage, https://www.tyollisyysrahasto.fi/en/benefits-for-adult-students/ (accessed on 22 July 2019). [9]

FiBS/DIE (2013), *Developing the adult learning sector. Annex to the final report*, FiBS/DIE, Berlin, http://lll.mon.bg/uploaded_files/financingannex_en.pdf (accessed on 30 July 2019). [11]

Finnish Government (2019), *Inclusive and competent Finland - a socially, economically and ecologically sustainable society*, Publication of the Finnish Government, Helsinki, http://julkaisut.valtioneuvosto.fi/bitstream/handle/10024/161664/Inclusive%20and%20compet ent%20Finland_2019.pdf?sequence=7&isAllowed=y (accessed on 8 July 2019). [3]

Kauhanen, A. (2018), "Yksilön, yrityksen ja yhteiskunnan vastuu työuranaikaisessa kouluttautumisessa [The responsibility of the individual, company and society for continuous learning in working life]", No. 67, ETLA Muistio, Helsinki, https://pub.etla.fi/ETLA-Muistio-Brief-67.pdf. [8]

Kela (2019), *Quick guide to financial aid for students - kela.fi*, Kela webpage, https://www.kela.fi/web/en/students-quick-guide (accessed on 22 July 2019). [10]

Ministry of Education and Culture (2019), "Jatkuvan oppimisen kehittäminen - työryhmän väliraportti [Developing continuous learning - working party report]", Ministry of Education and Culture, Helsinki. [4]

Ministry of Education and Culture (2012), *Education and Research 2011–2016. A development plan*, Ministry of Education and Culture, Helsinki, http://ncee.org/wp-content/uploads/2017/01/Fin-non-AV-5-Finnish-Ministry-of-Education-and-Culture-Education-and-Research-development-plan-2011-2016.pdf (accessed on 25 April 2019). [6]

Ministry of Education and Culture (2008), *Education and research 2007-2012. Development Plan.*, Ministry of Education and Culture, Helsinki, http://julkaisut.valtioneuvosto.fi/bitstream/handle/10024/79103/opm11.pdf?sequence=1&isAllo wed=y (accessed on 25 April 2019). [5]

OECD (2001), *Thematic Review on Adult Learning. Finland. Country note.*, OECD, Paris, https://www.oecd.org/education/skills-beyond-school/2541579.pdf (accessed on 8 May 2019). [1]

Richard Desjardins (ed.) (2017), *Political Economy of Adult Learning Systems*, Bloomsbury Academic, London, New York. [2]

3 Making continuous learning provision fit for the future

Finland's continuous learning system offers a wide range of learning opportunities for adults at all skill levels. Provision is typically public or quasi-public and comes free of charge or at little cost to the individual. While many adults take part in continuous learning, provision could be better calibrated to help adults keep abreast with the transformations of the labour market. This chapter describes the current structure of the continuous learning provision in Finland, as well as its alignment with the changing skill needs of the labour market. It highlights the key challenges facing the current system and makes recommendations on how to tackle these, based on international evidence.

Introduction

There is no "one size fits all" approach when it comes to optimal adult learning provision. What kind of education and training opportunities should be made available to help adults keep abreast with the changes in the world of work depends on each country's skill profiles and skill demand. Differences across countries call for tailored, country-specific solutions.

Yet, some basic desirable features of future-ready adult learning provision can be identified for all countries. First, provision should be broad enough to serve participants at all skill levels and should be relevant both to individual needs and to the labour market. Second, provision should be based on good quality and timely information on changing skill needs and dynamically adjusted to respond to these changes. Third, the system should offer learning opportunities that are flexible in modes and time of delivery and compatible with work and family obligations. Finally, for those in work, provision should offer shorter micro-modular learning opportunities to enable truly continuous learning, rather than requiring extended periods away from the labour market to gain a full formal qualification at once.

Finland already has a vast array of learning opportunities that meet many of these criteria, yet there is room for improvement. This chapter discusses the existing structure of adult learning provision in Finland, highlights its key challenges and draws out recommendations based on international good practice.

The current system

Structure of adult learning provision

Adult learning provision in Finland encompasses basic and general education; vocational education; higher education and adult liberal education. With the exception of basic and general education, there is little distinction between adult and youth education. All formal education qualifications are assigned a competence level within the Finnish Qualification Framework (FiNQF).

Basic and general upper secondary education gives adults the opportunity to obtain formal degrees, such as the matriculation examination or completing the lower secondary curriculum (Table 3.1). It also allows adults who have already obtained these formal degrees to re-take individual subjects to improve their grades. Teaching is provided in upper secondary schools for adults (*Aikuislukio/ Vuxenutbildning*), but adults can also study alongside young people in regular upper secondary schools (*Lukio/ Gymnasiet*) or folk high schools. Basic qualifications are referenced at Level 2 of the FiNQF, while general upper secondary qualifications are referenced at Level 4 (Finnish National Agency for Education, 2018[1]).

Table 3.1. Types of basic and general adult education provision in Finland

Types of provision	Providers	Duration	Costs to participants	FiNQF level	Participants (2017)
Basic education qualification (and subject studies)	Upper Secondary Schools for Adults Vocational Schools Folk High Schools Adult Education Centres	2-4 years	Free of charge; exception are subject studies which can be charged (typically EUR 20-150 per year)	Level 2	4 160 participants (full qualification) 1 334 participants (subject studies)
General upper secondary qualification (and subject studies)	Upper Secondary Schools for Adults General Upper Secondary Schools Folk High Schools	1-3 years	Free of charge; exception are subject studies which can be charged (typically EUR 20-150 per year)	Level 4	6 915 participants (full qualification) 15 924 participants (subject studies)

Note: Data refers to all participants following the curriculum for adults, irrespective of age (i.e. includes those below 25 years of age).
Source: OECD elaboration, all data Statistics Finland.

Vocational education encompasses a wide range of provision for adult learners (Table 3.2). Since the 2018 VET reform, there is no longer a distinction between youth and adult VET. Every individual follows the same path to access provision. Individuals can obtain initial vocational education (IVET), as well as continuing and specialised vocational qualifications. All qualifications are competence-based, which allows for the recognition of prior skills and knowledge and the development of individual learning paths. There are several forms of provision leading to a qualification:

- IVET (*ammatillinen perustutkinto / yrkesinriktad grundexamenis*) is offered at upper secondary level and aims to equip individuals with the skills necessary to find employment, be a good member of society and pursue further studies. Learners can choose one of 43 vocational upper secondary qualifications. IVET has a typical duration of three years, although length can vary depending on prior skills and knowledge. The qualification is referenced at Level 4 of the FiNQF, at the same level as a general upper secondary degree.[1]

- Further vocational qualifications (*ammattitutkinto / yrkesexamina*) serve the further development of individuals who are already in the workforce. Individuals typically take part in preparatory training for the competence test in one of 65 further qualifications. Training courses have varying length, but qualifications are awarded to people who can display more advanced or specialist skills than those required in IVET. In contrast to IVET qualifications, preparatory training only conveys vocational and no general skills. The qualification is referenced at Level 4 of the FiNQF.

- Specialised vocational qualifications (*erikoisammattitutkinto /specialyrkesexamina*) are for individuals in working-life who hold highly advanced or multidisciplinary skills (Ministry of Education and Culture, 2019[2]). Individuals can take-part in preparatory training to take the competence test for one of 56 specialist vocational qualifications. These are referenced at Level 5 of the FiNQF, higher than IVET and further vocational qualifications.

Table 3.2. Types of adult vocational education in Finland

Types of provision	Providers	Duration	Costs to participants	FiNQF level	Participants (2017)
Initial vocational qualification	Vocational institutions	Depending on prior competence (typically 2-3 years)	Free of charge	Level 4	84 428 adults
Further vocational qualification	Vocational institutions	Depending on prior competence (typically 1-1.5 years)	Reasonable fees can be charged (typically < EUR 500)	Level 4	47 551 adults
Specialist vocational qualification	Vocational institutions	Depending on prior competence (typically 1-1.5 years)	Reasonable fees can be charged (typically < EUR 500)	Level 5	24 758 adults
Non-formal VET/ short-courses	Vocational institutions	Flexible	Reasonable fees can be charged (typically < EUR 500)	Not assigned	53 247 participants*
Labour market training	Vocational institutions Universities, UAS Adult education centres Folk high schools Private providers	Flexible	Free of charge	Not assigned	Qualifications: 5 418 adults Courses not leading to qualifications: 30 142 participants*

Note: Number of participants aged 25 and above; *all participants, including adults below the age of 25.
Source: OECD elaboration, all data Vipunen database and Statistics Finland.

In addition to these full qualifications, vocational education encompasses vocational training not leading to a qualification (non-formal). This includes learning in the context of labour market training for the unemployed, staff training ordered by employers, joint-purchase training ordered jointly by employers and the PES, and independent completion of modules or part-qualifications.

In VET, teaching takes place at VET providers run by (groups of) municipalities, state-owned institutions and foundations, which bring together municipalities and private organisations/companies. Providers require an authorisation licence to provide education and training by the MoEC. Provision can be school-based with dedicated blocks of on-the-job learning or delivered in the form of apprenticeship training. Apprenticeship training allows individuals to complete a qualification while working. Apprenticeship training is the more popular training option for adults over 25 years of age (Kumpulainen, 2016[3]).

Higher education institutions are in principle open to all learners, irrespective of age and experience. Exceptions are some Master courses at Universities of Applied Sciences, which require work experience to enter. Higher education institutions include Universities (*yliopisto / universitet*), of which they are 13 specified in the Universities Act (558/2009) and 23 Universities of Applied Sciences (UAS, *ammattikorkeakoulu / yrkeshögskola*), which hold an operating license by the MoEC. While education at universities is research-driven, UAS have a strong practice orientation and ties with working life. Work-placements constitute an integral part of UAS studies. A recent law change obliges universities to offer continuing learning opportunities. Adults can take part in higher education in four ways:

1. Entering regular bachelor's and master's degree studies, through which adults can take modules or full degree programmes free of charge. UAS in particular see adults as one of their key target groups. In total, 76 000 of adults aged 25 or above were registered in Bachelor and Master courses at Universities and 77 000 at UAS. Half of 'adult' Bachelor students at Universities had signed-up for the course before the age of 25, while one in four of 'adult' Master students did the same. It is likely that these are 'initial' rather than adult learners, although the exact share is difficult to assess.

2. Each University or UAS also runs courses via Open Studies, based on each's institutions higher education syllabus. The aim of Open Studies is to provide individuals with opportunities to familiarise themselves with higher education, complement prior degrees or obtain new competencies (Ministry of Education and Culture, 2019[4]). Open Studies do not lead to qualifications, yet constitute parts of higher education degrees and offer an entryway into regular degree studies at Universities, typically after acquiring 60 credits under the European Credit Transfer system (ECTS) depending on the higher education institution. Traditionally the domain of adult learners, the lower age limit of 25 was abolished in the 1990s. This has led to an influx of mostly younger adults below the age of 30, who often participate with the intention to increase their chances of gaining a regular degree study place (Jauhiainen, Nori and Alho-Malmelin, 2007[5]; OECD, 2001[6]). Provision is modular, flexible and can be online. Participation is charged at a maximum of EUR 15 per ECTS credit.

3. Specialisation studies were introduced in 2015, as a new form of non-formal learning opportunities that are developed in cooperation with employers. Their purpose is to provide learning opportunities where there is no market-based offer (Ministry of Education and Culture, 2019[4]). Courses cover topics such as 'Big Data Analytics' or 'Music Management'. They target working adults who hold a higher education degree or equivalent skill levels. These learning opportunities are longer programmes equivalent to a minimum of 30 ECTS credits. Individuals are charged EUR 120 per credit.

4. In-service training/continuing professional education, which is developed for specific employers and 100% covered through employer contributions.

The resulting qualifications from higher education are categories at Levels 6 (Bachelor's degrees), 7 (Master's degrees) and 8 (Doctorate, Licentiate and specialised medical degrees) of the FiNQF (Finnish National Agency for Education, 2018[1]). Open Studies, Specialisation Studies and In-service Training does not lead to qualifications.

Table 3.3. Types of adult higher education in Finland

Types of provision	Providers	Duration	Cost to participants	FiNQF level	Participants (2017)
Bachelor's degree	Universities, UAS	3 years (University) 3.5-4 years (UAS)	Free of charge	Level 6	U: 32 359 adults UAS: 64 651 adults
Master's degree	Universities, UAS	2 years (University) 1-1.5 years (UAS)	Free of charge	Level 7	U: 43 690 adults UAS: 12 195 adults
Open Studies	Universities, UAS	Flexible	Max. EUR 15 / credit	Not assigned	U: 96 582 participants* UAS: 27 928 participants*
Professional specialisation studies	Universities, UAS	Flexible, at least 30 ECTS	Max. EUR 120 / credit	Not assigned	U: 5 450 participants* UAS: 1 071 adults
In-service training	Universities, UAS	Flexible	Free of charge, paid by employer	Not assigned	n/a

Note: Number of participants aged 25 and above; *all participants, including adults below the age of 25.
Source: OECD elaboration, all data Vipunen database and Statistics Finland.

Adult Liberal Education has a strong tradition in Finland. The first institutions were founded in the 19th century as grassroots institutions free from governmental control. Since then, the links between these institutions and the government have strengthened, not least through significant amounts of public funding. The landscape of adult liberal education providers is diverse and includes Adult Education Centres (*Kansalaisopisto*), Folk High School (*Kansanopisto*), Study Centres (*Opintokeskus*) and Summer Universities (*Kesäyliopisto*). The courses offered in these institutions are non-formal and typically related to recreation, citizenship and community development, although they increasingly include courses to develop basic and job-related skills for specific target groups. In 2018, Finnish liberal adult education was assigned the role of providing basic and literacy training for migrants. Participation in courses at adult liberal education institutions are recognised in the competence-based VET qualifications and validations of prior learning. Participants pay mostly small course fees, and specific target groups, e.g. migrants, receive training vouchers to participate in learning at adult liberal education institutions. While gross participation numbers in adult liberal education are around 1.5 million per year, it is estimated that the number of unique participants is 900 000.

Table 3.4. Types of adult liberal education in Finland

Providers	Duration	Cost to participants	FiNQF level	Participants (2017)
Adult Education Centres	Flexible	Small registration and participation fee, depending on municipality	Not assigned	1 055 486 participants*
Folk High Schools		Folk high school: Average around EUR 1 500/semester, 3 000/year Summer University: average 65 EUR/credit		104 469 participants*
Summer Universities				48 801 participants*
Study Centres				218 112 participants*
Vocational institutes				41 879 participants*

Note: *all participants, including adults below the age of 25.
Source: OECD elaboration, all data Vipunen database and Statistics Finland.

Every year, more than 1 million adults in Finland take part in **staff training** subsidised by their employer, according to data from the Adult Education Survey. 83% of companies with staff of 10 people or more are offering training opportunities, according to CVTS data. Smaller companies are less likely to do so. Staff training is training provided by employers for the development of their employees, some of which overlaps with the public provision mentioned above, e.g. formal and non-formal vocational training, in-service training provided by universities. It can also be provided by in-house trainers or purchased in the open market. Employers are obliged by law to draw up personnel and training plans for their company (Ministry of Labour, 2007[7]; Ministry of the Interior, 2007[8]). In companies with more than 30 employees, this must include principles for the provision of job-related coaching or training (Ministry of Labour, 2007[7]).

A form of staff training specific to the Finnish context is Joint Purchase Training (*Yhteishankintakoulutus/ Gemensam anskaffning av utbildning*), which is organised jointly by the PES and individual or groups of employers. The MoEE estimates that 3000-4000 people take part in training organised as joint-purchase training every year. Three types of training are available (OECD, 2017[9]; Eurofound, 2018[10]; OECD, 2019[11]):

- Recruitment Training (*RekryKoulutus/ RekryteringsUtbildning*) is the most popular form of Joint Purchase Training. It is organised with employers who struggle to find employees with the right skills. The PES supports the employer(s) in developing tailored training programmes, selecting a training provider and recruiting participants. Training duration is typically between 3 and 9 months, with a minimum requirement of 10 days, and should lead to a qualification that allows the individual to perform the required job. Training-costs are co-funded by the PES at a rate of 30%.
- Tailored Training (*TäsmäKoulutus/ PrecisionsUtbildning*) supports employers who want to retrain staff in order to adapt their skills to a changing operational or technological context of the company. The minimum training duration is 10 days, which can take place during time of temporary lay-off. The PES supports the company in selecting the education provider and employees eligible for training. It also co-funds the training by 50-70% depending on company size.
- Change Training *(MuutosKoulutus/ OmställningsUtbildning)* is organised in case of staff redundancies and supports workers to transition to new jobs. Training can last between 10 days and two years, with the view of obtaining a (partial) vocational degree. The PES co-funds 80% of the training costs.

The incoming Rinne government has pledged to increase the number of joint purchased trainings in the 2019-23 legislative period (Finnish Government, 2019[12]).

Table 3.5. Types of staff training in Finland

Types of provision	Providers	Duration	Costs to participants	FiNQF level	Participants (2017)
Courses commissioned by employers	Vocational schools UAS Folk high schools	Flexible	Free of charge	Not assigned	143 572 adults*
Joint-purchase training	Adult education centres Study circles Summer universities Private providers	Flexible	Free of charge	Not assigned	3 000-4 000 adults

Notes: *public provision only, all participants, including adults below the age of 25, excludes provision at sports institutes.
Source: OECD elaboration, all data Vipunen database, data provided by the Ministry of Economic Affairs and Employment.

Responsiveness of provision to labour market needs

In line with the Nordic tradition of adult education, adult learning in Finland aims to promote individual enjoyment and self-development according to individual interests and preferences, alongside developing competences in line with labour market needs (EAEA, 2011[13]).

Today, the vast majority of adults who participate in learning in Finland do so for job-related reasons such as to improve their career prospects or to improve their chances of finding a new job[2]. Various exercises exist to anticipate the skill needs of the labour market and align education provision with these skill needs.

Box 3.1. Training in the context of Active Labour Market Policies

The type of training taken up by job seekers registered with the PES (TE in Finland) has changed considerably over the past decade. In the past, the majority of adults taking part in training-focused Active Labour Market policies (ALMPs) participated in labour market training (Figure 3.1). Labour market training encompasses a range of training such as vocational short courses; standard initial, further or specialist vocational qualifications; vocational qualification modules; and entrepreneurship training. Employment and Economic Development Offices purchase the training from education providers and companies. Participation is free for the individual.

Since its introduction in 2009, self-motivated studies have become an increasingly popular option for job seekers (Figure 3.1). Self-motivated studies allow job seekers above the age of 25 to pursue a degree at a regular education institution full-time, while they continue to receive unemployment benefits. Job seekers can take-up self-motivated studies if the TE office agrees on the need and relevance of the training to improve job seekers' skills and employability. The unemployment benefit itself is paid by the Social Insurance Institution KELA or an unemployment fund.

These changes have led to an increased use of the regular adult learning system for training in the context of ALMPs. It implies a decrease in central control exerted by the Public Employment Services concerning the types of training that are made available to job seekers. In turn, individual caseworkers now make decisions on the admission to self-motivated studies on a case-by-case basis.

In recent years, both labour market training and self-motivated studies have increasingly been taken-up by migrants in the context of integration training.

Figure 3.1. Self-motivated studies are now dominating the ALMP training offer

Participants in ALMPs by type of programme, in thousands, 2006-18

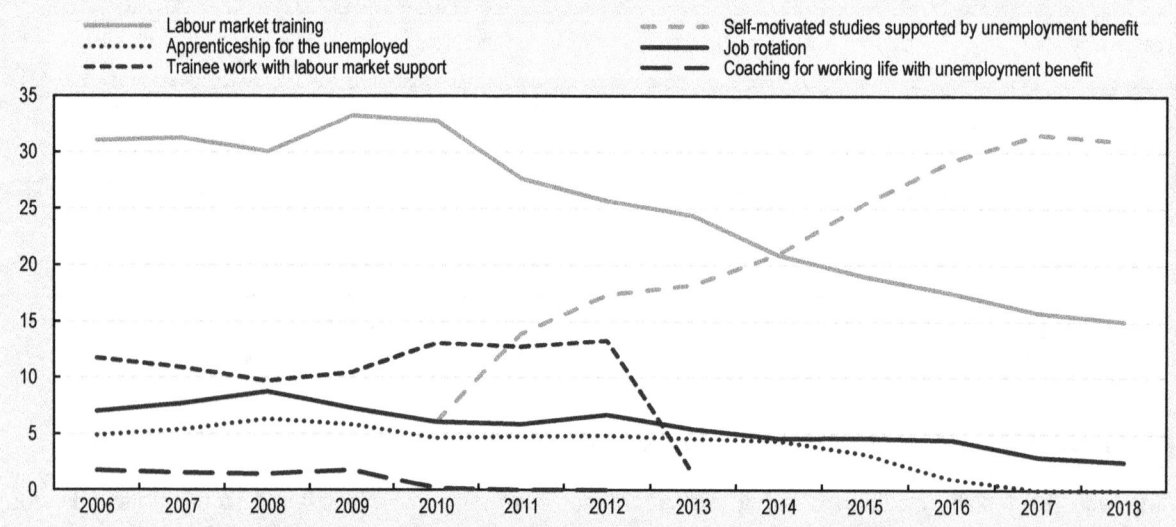

Note: Data refers to participants, not new entrants to ALMP training. It should be noted that self-motivated studies are typically of longer duration than labour market training and can stretch over several years.
Source: Ministry of Economic Affairs and Employment.

Anticipating the skill needs of the labour market

Finland has a long tradition of anticipating the skill needs of the labour market to inform policy-making and has been generating quantitative skill forecasts since the 1950s (Berge, Berg and Holm, 2015[14]). A great wealth of anticipation tools and processes are employed throughout the country, focusing on different governance levels, using different methods and time-horizons (OECD, 2016[15]). The system has been criticised for being too fragmented in the past, although recent efforts have aimed to streamline some of the anticipation exercises (Arnkill, 2010[16]).

The National Foresight Network brings together public and private actors involved in the anticipation of the key challenges and opportunities Finland is facing. It is run by the Prime Minister's Office and Sitra, the Finnish Innovation Fund (Nyyssölä, 2019[17]). Participants include regional councils, agencies, universities, researchers, companies, NGOS, as well as a range of different ministries, including the MOF, MoEE, MoEC and MHSA. These four ministries also finance the long-term structural forecast exercise conducted by the Government Institute for Economic research (VATT) using the VATTAGE general equilibrium model of the Finnish economy (Honkatukia, 2009[18]). Ministries use the results of this exercise as input to their own anticipation exercises.

At a national level, the Finnish National Agency of Education (EDUFIN), a subsidiary of the MoEC, uses the VATT structural forecast as basis of their education and skill anticipation exercise. The anticipation process is currently in transition, as it consolidates the previously separate qualitative (VOSE-model) and quantitative anticipation exercises (Mitenna-model) into one single 'basic anticipation process' (Box 3.2).

Box 3.2. The new 'Basic Anticipation Process'

Since 2017, the **new National Forum for Skill Anticipation (*Osaamisen ennakointifoorumi*)** serves as an expert body for skill anticipation and coordinates sector-specific anticipation groups. Nine anticipation groups are responsible for the anticipation of competence and skill needs in their specific sector, the development of recommendations to improve education and training and the conduct of further research. Each anticipation group is composed of the social partners, representatives of educational providers, trade unions of teaching staff, researchers and members of the education administration. The nine sectors covered are natural resources, food production and the environment; business and administration; education, culture and communications; transport and logistic; hospitality services; built environment; social, health and welfare services; technology industry and services; process industry and production. Anticipation groups draw on a wide range of experts in the anticipation process.

The anticipation process involves a series of five workshops, supported by preparatory exchanges on electronic platforms and a series of background studies. The VATT industry forecasts estimating workforce demand until 2035 is one of the key inputs to the exercise and is adjusted using qualitative information. Key outputs of the workshops are scenarios for the development of the employment, industrial and occupational structure, as well as competence, skill and educational needs arising from these. EDUFIN's foresight unit translates these insights into quantitative estimates of educational needs. The first results of the 'basic anticipation process' were published in early 2019. In addition, EDUFIN supports regional anticipation exercises carried out by regional councils.

Source: Nyyssölä (2019[17]), "The Finnish Anticipation System"; Finnish National Agency for Education (2017[19]), "The anticipation plan of the National Forum for Skills Anticipation"; Finnish Board of Education (2019[20]), Osaaminen 2035 – Osaamisen ennakointifoorumin ensimmäisiä ennakointituloksia [Expertise 2035 – First Foresight Results from the Foresight Forum], www.oph.fi.

On the employment side, the MoEE publishes short-term labour market forecasts twice yearly in spring and autumn. The basis for these forecasts are labour market, demographic and national account statistics, the economic forecast by the Ministry of Finance, recruitment tracking data and regional economic surveys (Alatalo, Larja and Mähönen, 2019[21]). It provides forecasts for short-term overall labour demand, as well as demand in the broad sectors of the economy.

At a regional level, most regions carry out their own skill anticipation exercises bringing together different stakeholders in anticipation committees. Centres for Economic Development, Transport and the Environment (*ELY centres*) and the Employment and Economic Development Offices (*TE offices*) play a key role in these processes. ELY centres have the responsibility for matching skill demand and supply and the anticipation of continuous learning needs. Skill anticipation exercises conducted by ELY centres are typically short-term. TE-offices also conduct employer surveys on behalf of ELY centres (Berge, Berg and Holm, 2015[14]). A key tool is the Occupational Barometer (*ammattibarometri*), which forecasts short-term occupational needs at the regional level. The barometer summarises the views of the TE offices about the employment prospects of 200 key occupations in the coming 6 months, based on employer visits and interviews with employer and employees. The results of this exercise are publicly available.[3]

In addition, vocational and higher educational institutions are required by law to conduct anticipation activities (Skills Panorama, 2017[22]). These exercises typically involve labour market representatives. Some institutions are making use of AI in these anticipation exercises (see Box 3.3).

Box 3.3. Using artificial intelligence to anticipate skill needs

The Helsinki Metropolitan Universities of Applied Sciences[1] collaborate with Headai Ltd., a for-profit organisation specialised in artificial intelligence (AI), to analyse the gap between the skill needs of the labour market and their education offer.

Headai uses AI (natural language processing algorithms) to analyse job advertisements and extract real-time information on the demand for skills in the labour market. This information is then compared to the skills conveyed in existing education programmes, extracted from curricula and study programmes using the same technology. Both skill demand and the skills supplied through existing education programmes are visualised in competence maps. These maps are also useful to compare the skill content of different education programmes.

The institutions aim to use this data to: i) Understand current and future skill demand; ii) Provide information and guidance to students on course selection and individual learning paths; iii) Shape curriculum development; iv) Make the education offer more competitive; and v) Develop competences of university staff.

Headai received the Ratkaisu 100 Challenge Price in 2017 for its innovative work on skill mapping, which was awarded by the Finnish Innovation Fund Sitra.

1. An alliance of the three Universities of Applied Sciences: Haaga-Helia, Laurea and Metropolia.
Source: Ketamo et al. (2019[23]), "Mapping the Future Curriculum: Adopting Artifical Intelligence and Analytics in Forecasting Competence Needs", http://urn.fi/URN:NBN:fi-fe2019053117966; Headai (2019[24]), "Customer Story: Helsinki Metropolitan Universities of Applied Sciences", https://medium.com/headai-customer-stories/customer-story-3amk-4f7944080344; Sitra (2019[25]), "How can we predict what expertise will be needed in the future? Artificial intelligence knows – Sitra", https://www.sitra.fi/en/articles/can-predict-expertise-will-needed-future-artificial-intelligence-knows/; Sitra (2017[26]), "Artificial intelligence shows what Finland can do and a positive CV reveals the hidden talents of young people: The winners of Sitra's million-euro Ratkaisu 100 Challenge competition", https://www.sitra.fi/en/news/artificial-intelligence-shows-finland-can-positive-cv-reveals-hidden-talents-young-people-winners-sitras-100-million-euro-ratkaisu-100-challenge-competition/.

Using anticipation information to shape adult learning provision

Skill anticipation information can be used to influence the behaviour of individuals, providers and employers to take-part in and offer learning opportunities in line with skill demands (OECD, 2019[11]). Typical instruments include information provision, setting adapted financial incentives and regulating the education and training provision in line with labour market needs.

Information from skill anticipation exercises is made available to the public through reports, websites and other communication tools. In theory, this information can be used by individuals to make informed choices about engaging in learning, which enables them to gain skills that are in demand in the labour market. In reality, policy-makers and professionals, such as career guidance staff in TE-centres, are the primary users of this information. There are ongoing initiatives within the MoEE and MoEC to make this information available online in a more user-friendly format.

Many countries use **financial incentives** to steer educational choices (OECD, 2017[9]). The Finnish tradition of public, universal and free or low-cost adult learning provision currently limits the instruments available to steer educational provision and take-up (see challenges below). Most adult learning provision is currently free of charge or available at low-cost to the individual. Course costs are not currently used to incentivise or dis-incentivise the take-up of adult learning opportunities in line with skill demand. An exception is the use of training vouchers for specific groups in adult liberal education, which pays for (part of) their training costs. However, the link to skill anticipation is limited, as the vouchers are typically not tied to specific education and training courses. Similarly, the availability of financial support to the livelihood of individuals during their studies (adult education allowance, scholarship for qualified employees, financial aid for students) is not tied to the labour-market relevance of the pursued training option. Exceptions are the financial support options provided to unemployed individuals who take up training (social assistance for the unemployed in training, self-study allowance), as TE-offices solely support labour-market relevant training for the unemployed. The judgement of labour-market relevance is typically based on a case-by-case decision of a career counsellor.

Skill anticipation information plays a role in the **regulation of education and training provision**. At a national level, results of the EDUFI anticipation exercises inform the planning of educational provision to some extent. In the past, forecast results have been used in the preparation of the Education Development plans (Berge, Berg and Holm, 2015[14]), yet no such plans were developed in recent years. When they existed, forecast results and targets set in development plans were never fully aligned (Hanhijoki et al., 2012[27]). The most recent anticipation exercise by the Skill Anticipation Forum suggests wide reaching reforms of the continuous learning system and that resources should be transferred from formal education to (non-formal) continuous education. It remains to be seen if and how the incoming government will implement these recommendations (Finnish National Agency of Education, 2019[28]).

More generally, skill anticipation exercises inform the quantity of educational provision as they are taken into account when setting admission targets for vocational education, granting operating licenses for VET and higher education providers and when negotiating the scope of educational provision with universities (Hanhijoki et al., 2012[27]). Results also influence the content of provision as EDUFI uses the results to develop qualifications, curricula and teaching contents for vocational qualifications. Beyond using skill anticipation information directly, recent reforms have strengthened the systemic mechanisms that align formal training with labour market needs. Funding for VET and higher education institutions is now tied to labour-market related indicators such as the employment rate of graduates.

At the regional level, the Occupational Barometer and other anticipation exercises by the ELY-centres and TE-offices are used by career guidance counsellors and in the commissioning of labour market training. Education providers increasingly use information from their own skill anticipation exercises to shape provision (Berge, Berg and Holm, 2015[14]).

Key challenges

Finland has a wide array of learning opportunities for adults. Yet, they could be better calibrated to help individuals gain the relevant skills for a changing labour market in a more efficient way. Key challenges relate to: greater incentives for participation in formal learning than non-formal learning; the existence of some specific gaps in the provision; and the limited alignment with labour market needs.

The existing structure favours formal over non-formal learning.

Formal qualifications are highly valued in the Finnish labour market and society. Finnish adults (25-64) have the highest formal learning participation of any European country and are 2.5 times more likely to take part in formal education than the EU-average (14.2% vs. 5.8%). While formal learning participation has decreased in Europe over the past decade, it has significantly increased in Finland.

Some of this can be explained by prolonged initial education careers in Finland, but even older age groups are twice as likely to participate in formal learning as their European counter-parts. Finland's existing adult learning provision promotes participation in formal learning: most formal education is open to adult learners; the completion of formal qualifications is generally free of charge; and financial support is available for those studying towards a qualification. By contrast, non-formal education offers are typically subject to a (small) fee and financial support to pursue them is more limited. It is perhaps unsurprising then that an increasing share of adults participate in formal education programmes that were initially conceived as initial education options for young people.

Bachelor's degree programmes, for example, are relatively lengthy programmes (3-4 years of full-time study) that are intended to allow individuals to gain a first academic qualification in a chosen field and access to the labour market. The share of adults aged 25+, who register for a Bachelor's degree ('new students') at higher education institutions, has steadily increased over the past 15 years (Figure 3.2). Some of the new starters already hold bachelor's degrees: this is the case for 18% of adults at UAS and 45% of adults at universities.

Figure 3.2. Adults increasingly pursue bachelor degrees at UAS

New bachelor students by age group, % of total new students

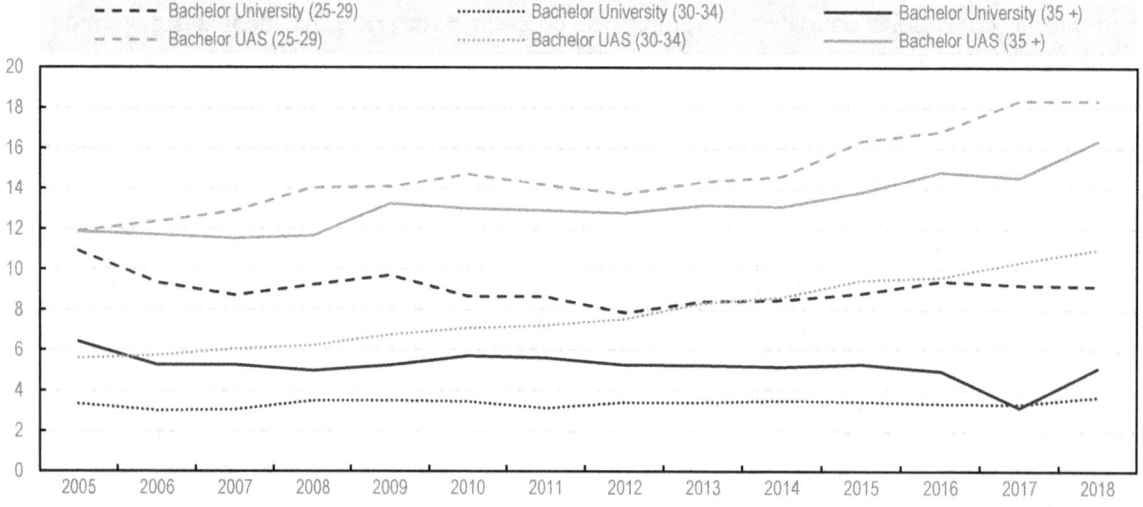

Note: New students refers to students registered for the first time with the institution as being present or absent in their degree programme. This includes students who are changing institution or course, i.e. are not new to higher education.
Source: Statistics Finland, Vipunen database.

Many adults have legitimate reasons to pursue a first tertiary degree later in life, because of, for example, not meeting entry criteria when they were younger or a lack of available study places. They may also want to acquire work experience first, before taking-up study towards a higher education degree. This is in particular the case for adults who take-up Bachelor degrees at UAS. However, the take-up of initial education opportunities by adults can point to in-efficiencies in the adult education system, particularly when adults obtain repeated formal degrees at the same level they already hold (e.g. repeated Bachelor degrees):

- Pursuing a lengthy initial vocational or higher education degree can help some adults with professional reorientation, for example, when they can no longer work in their initial profession due to health reasons or when their initial occupation is subject to widespread automation. Yet, in the majority of cases, pursuing a three to four year initial degree is not a time and resource efficient way to keep abreast with the changing skill needs of the labour market. The high and increasing take-up of initial education opportunities may point to a lack of other formal, non-formal and informal opportunities more suited to adults' needs.

- The lack of a distinction between adult and youth education may also have negative effects on the education opportunities of young people. Recent general upper secondary graduates can face waiting times of several years to get access to the highly restricted university places. Taking as an example the cohort of those who graduated with general upper secondary education in 2011, 77% applied to higher education in the year of graduation, yet only 38% were able to enter higher education in that year. 5-years after graduation, only 81% of the cohort had studied in higher education while 94% had applied. In the meantime, many choose to take part in fee-based Open University provision, which can give access to degree programmes at regular universities. Research from 2007 suggests that around 40% of students in Open Universities might be young people aiming to get a degree by transferring to a regular study programmes (Jauhiainen, Nori and Alho-Malmelin, 2007[5]). Anecdotal evidence indicates that the share of young people participating in Open University Studies has increased since then.

There are some important gaps in the continuous learning provision.

Need for shorter non-formal learning opportunities that are labour-market relevant.

Most adults need shorter, labour-market relevant learning opportunities that they can pursue alongside their work and family responsibilities. These opportunities allow adults to become effectively continuous learners over the life-course, rather than learners that take out substantial blocks of time to pursue further formal qualifications a few times in their lives. By contrast, formal learning is time and resource intensive, has limited returns (see Box 3.4) and does not necessarily lead to upskilling, e.g. in the case of working towards several qualifications at the same level.

Currently, job-related non-formal learning opportunities include provision at open universities/UAS, non-formal vocational training at VET schools, some limited job-related training opportunities at Adult Education Centres and Folk High Schools (e.g. photoshop, basics of accounting), as well as training organised by TE-offices and employers themselves. While these programmes are short in comparison to formal education, they are often organised in modules that still require significant time investment of individuals. Employers are advocating the development of short courses that equip individuals with specific labour market specific skills. The expectation is that these courses would be even shorter than the modular provision that already exists in some parts of the adult learning system.

Further, where non-formal learning opportunities are available, employers or public employment services typically moderate access to them. Opportunities that can be accessed by individuals on their own initiative and at their own (potentially subsidised) cost are also limited.

Lack of opportunities to gain higher vocational skills.

The majority of initial and further vocational training in Finland takes place at Level 4 of the European Qualification Framework, i.e. at a level equivalent to general upper secondary qualification. Only specialist vocational qualifications are categorised at Level 5 of the European Qualification Framework, although the level of these qualifications is considered low. Given the limited higher vocational development opportunities for adults with vocational degree, many pursue Bachelor's degrees at UAS to upskill. As described above, these are lengthy and may not be the most appropriate provision for adults with work-experience looking to qualify further.

Higher vocational post-secondary degrees have existed in Finland in the past, but disappeared when higher vocational colleges were transformed into polytechnics (later UAS). A key aim of the 'polytechnic experiment' of the 1990s was to channel the increasing demand for higher education to newly created polytechnics, rather than universities, and to diversify education provision (OECD, 2003[29]). At the same time, a reform of the university degree system introduced three-year Bachelor degrees at Polytechnics, which replaced shorter upper-secondary vocational degrees (OECD, 1999[30]).

These reforms upgraded the provision of many former higher vocational colleges to tertiary-level education, yet effectively abolished post-secondary non-tertiary education in Finland (with the exception of specialist vocational qualifications). Adults with vocational degrees now have limited options for up-skilling beyond taking three-year bachelor degrees and specialist vocational qualifications.

The use of skills anticipation information for the steering of education provision is limited.

Good information on skill needs is important both for steering the provision and take up of education and training. Finland has an abundance of skills anticipation exercises at all levels of governance, yet it has been argued that their link to policy-making could be stronger (Kaivo-Oja and Marttinen, 2008[31]; OECD, 2016[15]; Berge, Berg and Holm, 2015[14]). The exact mechanisms by which skills anticipation information feeds into policy design often remain unclear. Some stakeholders seem to believe that the information automatically translates into education provision, for example by virtue of the National Agency of Education being responsible for both skills anticipation and the formulation of qualifications and curricula. In reality, formal mechanisms to link both are often lacking. A notable exception are the training activities organised by the ELY-centres, which are designed to respond to the short-term skill needs identified in regional anticipation exercises.

Even where skills anticipation exercises are consulted, adult education providers have significant freedom to shape the quantity and content of the education offer. Following licencing and agreements with the MoEC, providers can transfer admission numbers between different fields if this stays within the overall numbers specified.

Perhaps most importantly, the public, universal and free nature of much adult learning provision constitutes a key challenge to the use of skill anticipation information in the steering of educational choices by individuals. While other countries use financial incentives to steer individual demand towards specific courses, e.g. by lowering tuition fees for university programmes for skills in demand, such mechanisms are not currently possible in the Finnish context of free adult education.

Box 3.4. Wage returns to training

While participation in adult learning in Finland is high, there is only limited evidence that it leads to positive labour market outcomes. Recent evidence from OECD research suggests that the wage returns to learning participation are modest (Fialho, Quintini and Vandeweyer, 2019[32]). In Finland, participation in non-formal learning is associated with 7% higher wages, while participation in informal and formal learning is associated with lower wages (-2% and -1% respectively). Other Nordic countries see similar returns to non-formal learning, but participation in informal learning is associated with higher wages. These effects are correlations and should not be interpreted as causal.

These findings are in line with national research on the effects of take-up of the education leave subsidy, which is used during long-absences from work for the purpose of obtaining formal qualifications (Kauhanen, 2018[33]). It finds that while participation substantially increases educational attainment, it has a negative effect on employment and earnings not only during the lock-in period, but also up to four years after take-up of the subsidy. An exception to these findings concerns participation in polytechnic education. Research suggests that adults aged 25+ who attend polytechnic education have significantly higher earnings and employment rates than comparable adults without a tertiary degree. Ten years after starting a polytechnic degree, earnings are close to EUR 4 000 per year higher than those of the comparison group (Böckerman, Haapanen and Jepsen, 2017[34]).

Figure 3.3. Participation in formal and informal adult learning are associated with lower wages

Returns to training by country, % wage increase

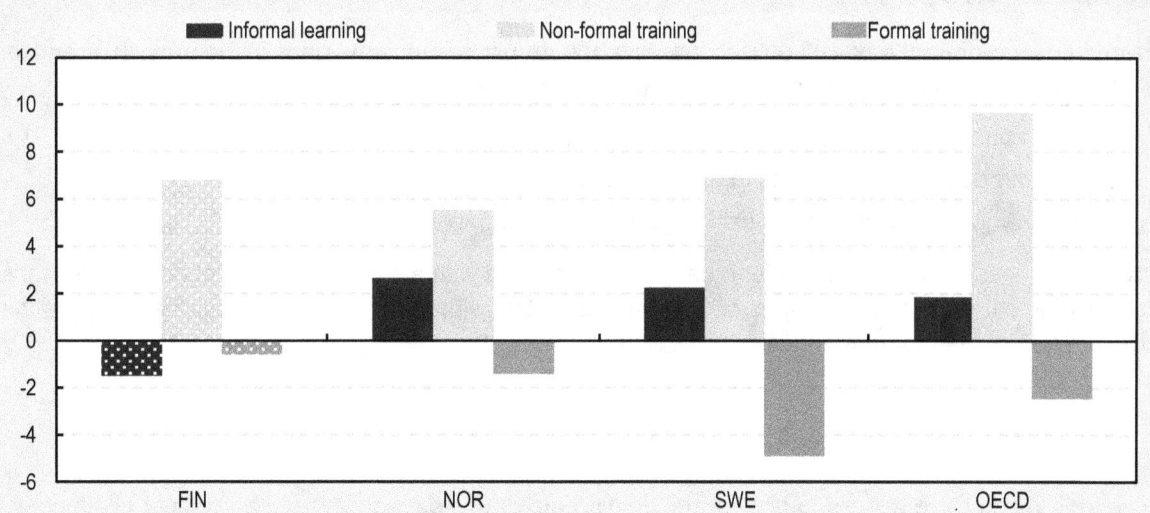

Note: Job-related formal and non-formal training are computed based on workers who report that the latest training activity was job-related.
Source: Fialho, Quintini and Vandeweyer, (2019[32]), Returns to different forms of job-related training: Factoring in informal learning, https://doi.org/10.1787/1815199X, based on PIAAC (2012, 2015).

As returns are measured a relatively short time-period after training in Fialho, Quintini and Vandeweyer (2019[32]), further positive effects may occur later or may require a job-move to materialise. This is particularly true for Finland, a country with high wage compression and a high share of public sector workers. Results may also reflect differences in quality and labour-market relevance of training across countries, as well as shares of workplaces that apply High Performance Work-organisation Practices (HPWP) as these are typically associated with higher returns to training.

Policy recommendations and good practices

Recommendation

Before implementing any specific policy recommendations, Finland should develop an overarching vision for its continuous learning system. This would include how different types of provision contribute to the whole and a review of the linkages of the adult learning system and other policy areas, such as initial education, wage setting, health care or social security, as there are important interaction effects between them. This would help to prioritise the action that should be taken and identify complementary measures that would increase the effectiveness of the proposed policy reforms. Therefore, Finland may wish to:

1. Develop a joined-up strategy for a future-ready system of continuous learning.

To address the specific challenges identified above, Finland should consider: i) diversifying the training offer; ii) making the training offer more labour-market relevant; and iii) incentivising individuals to take part in the 'right' offer. In each of these areas, Finland could draw on international examples of good practice. This should be part of an overall vision for reform of Finland's continuous learning system.

Diversify the training offer

Recommendations

Finland has a wide-range of well-utilised learning opportunities, but some gaps in the provision remain. In particular, the Finnish continuous learning system could benefit from:

1. An expansion of the non-formal training offer;
2. Re-introducing opportunities to gain higher vocational skills;
3. Exploring the introduction of short-cycle tertiary education.

Any diversification of the training offer must go hand-in-hand with a clear placement of new offers in the current Finnish qualification system and be implemented with the goal of keeping the qualification structure transparent for individuals.

Improving the market for non-formal training.

Giving individuals more access to non-formal training opportunities, addresses several key challenges of the Finnish system. Non-formal learning opportunities are specifically directed at (working) adults. If properly designed, funded and quality assured, they have the potential to ensure that adults do not crowd out initial training opportunities designed for young people. They also have the potential to be short and labour-market relevant, specifically when designed with the strong involvement of employers. These learning opportunities would enable adults to update their skills continuously over the life-course, while being compatible with their work and family responsibilities Shorter non-formal training would also reduce the payback time to make the investment in training worthwhile.

Improving the market for non-formal training options and incentivising the take-up of such options is a complex undertaking. The functioning of the current market for labour-market relevant short courses may require radical solutions to shift away from the status quo. The change requires rethinking the funding for non-formal provision and experimenting with more market-based solutions. In a qualification-driven education system such as Finland, it also necessitates the development of certification systems for non-formal short-courses and a determination of how these non-formal courses relate to formal qualifications, e.g. by constituting micro building blocks of formal qualifications.

It is likely that Finland will build on its tradition of open, universal and free or low-cost provision, when it comes to the expansion of non-formal training opportunities. Consideration must therefore be given to how public and, more importantly, private providers can be incentivised to offer non-formal training opportunities, while keeping costs low for individuals. The recent Working Group on Continuous Learning (Ministry of Education and Culture, 2019[35]) explored different funding options for continuous learning provision, without recommending a specific solution due to political differences. Key ways in which non-formal training provision could be expanded and made more market-based include:

- **Public procurement in open calls for tender**: This involves the public funding of non-formal training provision, following a public procurement process and selection of public and/or private providers. Providers deliver education and training in line with a contractual agreement with the responsible ministries, which specify performance targets and related funding. Estonia, for example, has been offering short-term non-formal vocational courses free of charge since 2009. Since then, approximately 75 000 adults have taken part in these courses, which is approximately 10% of the Estonian adult population aged 25-64. Courses provide training opportunities in line with labour market needs, comprise between 20 and 100 academic hours and are free of charge to the individual. Providers are currently vocational and higher professional education institutions, which are selected in yearly calls for tenders issued by the Ministry of Education. While the non-formal training offer has led to positive labour market outcomes for individuals (Leetma et al., 2015[36]), it should be noted that the state-funded provision has essentially crowded out private providers of non-formal learning. This could be addressed by opening the calls to private providers meeting specified quality criteria.

- **Voucher schemes** cut out the governmental procurement process and directly link funding for providers to the training choices made by individuals. In the countries using vouchers, individuals are given vouchers by the responsible ministries that can be used to cover part or all of the direct training costs. Training providers receive funding when the individual signs-up and/or complete a training course. Vouchers schemes can be used for both public and private providers meeting certain quality criteria and hence can incentivise a market of non-formal training provision. In Germany, for example, training vouchers (*Bildungsprämie*) are available for employed individuals on low-incomes, as well as individuals who are on care leave (BMAS, 2019[37]). These vouchers can be used for job-related vocational or basic education, language and ICT training at education and training providers that meet specified quality criteria. The vouchers cover 50% of the training costs, up to EUR 500. Individuals must take part in career guidance counselling at one of 530 guidance centres before getting access to the voucher. Finland has experience of using a voucher-based approach for liberal adult education courses, yet these currently do not cover private providers and only cover very specific groups of adults.

- **Individual learning accounts** link funding of providers to training choices made by individuals. Individuals can typically accumulate rights to training/resources in their account over time, which are then mobilised when training is undertaken (OECD, 2019[38]). Providers are paid when the individual takes up training and/or completes their course. The French Individual Learning Account Scheme (*Compte Personnel de Formation*) allows individuals aged 16+ to accumulate up to EUR 500 per year in 'training rights' in their individual account up to a ceiling of EUR 5 000. Thresholds for adults with low-skills (below ISCED 3) are higher with EUR 800 per year and EUR 8 000/overall. Credits are transferable between employers and are maintained if labour market status changes. Training rights can only be used towards recognised qualifications or basic skill training. A similar model could be implemented for the participation in non-formal training, if implemented alongside sufficient quality assurance mechanisms.

To make non-formal learning an attractive training choice for individuals, the training offer must be of high quality. Currently, public providers are responsible for ensuring the quality of their provision with the support of FINEEC. In the context of introducing more market-based mechanisms, more complex quality assurance mechanisms, such as accreditation of providers and the introduction of a certification system for non-formal short-courses, must be considered. Many countries are grappling with the issue of quality assurance of adult education. Austria introduced the national quality assurance system Ö-Cert in 2011 to improve transparency in the very heterogeneous market of an estimated 1 800 to 3 000 adult learning providers in Austria. While Finland would start from the opposite end of the spectrum with a limited number of adult learning providers, there are important lessons from the basic quality requirements set in Austria. To obtain the Ö-Cert certification, providers must meet basic requirements regarding: i) the corporate mission and responsibility; ii) their organisational structure and staff competences; iii) the nature of courses offered; iv) a commitment to ethical principles and democracy; and v) the existence of an approved quality management system. Quality is assessed by submitting a quality certificate by any of the Ö-Cert approved certification providers (EPALE, 2019[39]; Bundesministeriums für Bildung, 2017[40]).

Certification systems should be developed with strong employer involvement to achieve buy-in and labour-market relevance. One way to achieve this is by giving employer organisations the responsibility to certify non-formal training. In Germany, for example, the Chambers of Commerce and Industry (IHKs) are entrusted to certify shorter courses in their fields. An example from the retail industry is the Shop Manager Course, which covers higher level skills as it intends to train managers, but in a context that is closely related to a specific occupation and job role. Such courses are widely known and recognised by employers, therefore they provide pathways for career progression.

Re-introduce opportunities to develop higher vocational skills.

The transformation of higher vocational colleges into polytechnics and later Universities of Applied Sciences has left a gap in the provision for higher-level vocational skills (i.e. post-secondary, non-tertiary opportunities). Re-introducing such opportunities is critical in order to provide upskilling pathways for the approximately 40% of the Finnish population whose highest degree is a vocational degree and who wish to gain further vocational qualifications. In order to shift the entire skill distribution of the Finnish population upwards, it is essential that these opportunities allow people to upskill to higher levels, i.e. Level 5 and Level 6 of the National Qualification Framework, rather than solely obtaining further qualifications at the level already held. Diversifying the education and training offer at this level may also help to alleviate the pressure on the higher education system as the sole upskilling pathway after the upper secondary level.

Only a small number of countries offer higher vocational qualifications at EQF-level 6. These countries typically have strong dual VET systems, such as Austria, Germany and Switzerland. In Germany, advanced further training (*Aufstiegsfortbildung*) leads to 'Master craftsmen' qualifications. The precondition for participation is, similar to the specialist vocational qualifications in Finland, typically an initial vocational degree and work experience. It is not necessary to take part in an advanced further training to be admitted to take a 'Master craftsmen' qualification. The training qualifies individuals to take greater responsibility in the workplace and equips individuals with specific rights such as the right to open their own business or to train apprentices. Courses are provided by certified public or private education providers, as well as educational institutions of the Chambers of Commerce and Trade. The Chambers are also the responsible body for the award of the qualifications (Bundesministerium für Justiz und Verbraucherschutz, 2016[41]; Bundesministerium für Justiz und Verbraucherschutz, 2005[42]). The social partners and professional organisations are key players in the design, implementation and quality assurance of further training courses.

Switzerland provides upskilling opportunities at EQF Level 6 through its Professional Education and Training System (PET, *höhere Berufsbildung*). Professional Education prepares individuals for demanding occupational fields and leadership positions. Similar to Finland's dual tertiary sector with Universities and

Universities of Applied Sciences, the PET sector constitutes a parallel tertiary sector (Tertiary level B) next to the higher education system (Tertiary level A). PET training institutions can be public or private, as well as run by the social partners. They include professional colleges (*höhere Fachschulen*) and preparatory courses for National PET examinations (*Eidgenössische Berufsprüfung, höhere Fachprüfung*) (Fazekas and Field, 2013[43]). The social partners, professional organisations, federal and cantonal governments are key players of the PET system. The federal government has the responsibility for the overall development and quality assurance of the system; it also approves examination regulations of PET qualifications. Professional organisations define the content of qualifications and assessment criteria; they also provide PET training opportunities. The cantonal governments are responsible for the supervision of professional colleges and to some extent preparatory courses of National PET examinations. Social partners contribute to the further development of the system (Staatssekretariat für Bildung, 2017[44]; Fazekas and Field, 2013[43]). These qualifications play a significant role in the Swiss qualification landscape. According to the Federal Office for Statistics Switzerland, approximately 27 000 people gained a tertiary qualification through the PET system in 2018, close to the number of people who gained Bachelor-level degrees at universities and universities of applied sciences in that year (31 500).

It may be argued that the Finnish vocational system does not follow the same tradition as the dual VET systems of Austria, Germany and Switzerland, making it difficult to transfer their practices. While some aspects are indeed embedded in their specific national contexts, it should be noted that Finland used to have a system of higher vocational qualifications in the past. With the former higher vocational colleges having been transformed, it is now worth considering which educational institutions could offer higher vocational programmes in the future. Most promising candidates are Vocational Schools, UAS or partnerships between both types of institutions. Key learning from good practices in other countries include: the leadership role of professional organisations in the design of these qualifications, the specification of added rights acquired through vocational upskilling (e.g. training apprentices), as well as the equivalent status of higher level vocational and academic Bachelor's degrees at Level 6 of the EQF.

Explore the introduction of short-cycle tertiary education.

While taking entire Bachelor degrees might be relevant to some adults, it is unlikely that this provision is relevant to the upskilling and reskilling needs of the vast majority. It is therefore good practice across OECD countries that the tertiary education offer includes practical-based short-cycle degrees to provide opportunities for those who do not have the time or inclination to take part in three-year bachelor degree courses. Some commentators have gone so far as to describe short-cycle tertiary courses as "the missing link" between secondary and higher education in Europe (Kirsch and Beernaert, 2011[45]).

The majority of OECD economies have short-cycle tertiary education as part of their educational offer (Kirsch and Beernaert, 2011[45]; Cremonini, 2010[46]). This includes Finland's Nordic neighbours Denmark and Norway. In Denmark, for example, nine Business and Technical Academies (*erhvervsakademier*, equivalent to UAS) offer short-cycle higher education programmes. These programmes are of 2-years duration (120 ECTS) and lead to the award of an academy professional degree (*erhvervsakademigrad, AK*). Graduates have the opportunity to convert this degree into a bachelor's degree with an additional year (60 ECTS) of study, i.e. through participation in a Top-up Bachelor degree programme. In Denmark, 18% of first-time tertiary graduates graduate with a short-cycle degree. Short-cycle graduates benefit from somewhat higher employment rates and relative earnings compared to graduates of Bachelor's degree programmes, likely due to their more practical orientation (OECD, 2018[47]).

Short-cycle tertiary education at ISCED Level 5 is defined as having a minimum 2-year duration (OECD, 2015[48]). However, some countries offer programmes of even shorter duration at tertiary level. The *Higher National Certificate* in the United Kingdom is a higher education qualification awarded after one year of full-time study. Study programmes aim to help individuals develop the skills required in a particular area of work. *Higher National Certificates* can constitute the first year of a two-year *Higher National Diploma* qualification, which itself can be expanded to a Bachelor's degree qualification after a third year of study. Further education colleges or higher education institutions offer study programmes. Around 13% of first time tertiary graduates graduate with a short-cycle tertiary degree in the UK (OECD, 2018[49]).

Finland itself has experimented with short-cycle tertiary study programmes in recent years. Between 2013 and 2016, the JAMK University of Applied Sciences ran a pilot project on short-cycle tertiary education funded by the MoEC (JAMK, 2019[50]). JAMK UAS offered four study programmes,[4] awarding a Diploma of Higher Education (*Korkeakouludiplomi*) after 1-year of full-time study (60 ECTS). As the programme was implemented in the context of Open UAS studies, participation did not lead to a degree, but could form the basis of a regular bachelor's degree. It was also subject to the regular fees for Open UAS study. Research on the pilot found that around half of the participants took part in the new programme to improve the skills and knowledge for their current job, while the other half took part in the programme as a stepping stone into degree study or to a career change. The evidence also suggests that the employment and wage impact of participation was clearly limited, as no formal qualifications were acquired (Aittola and Ursin, 2019[51]).

Based on the national and international experience, Finland should consider the introduction of short-cycle tertiary learning opportunities with the view to incentivising take-up of tertiary education of groups that would traditionally not do so. This includes the large share of Finns with vocational qualifications at FiNQF Levels 4 and 5. The introduction of short-cycle tertiary education may also ease the pressure on the initial Bachelor's degree education system, where individuals are solely looking to take tertiary-level courses rather than entire Bachelor's degrees. Learning from good practice, it will be essential to i) implement pilots on the introduction of short-cycle tertiary degrees; ii) reflect on the subject areas in which short-cycle tertiary degrees can provide added value to students and the labour market; iii) test the desirability of these study options for individuals and employers and iv) design transition pathways from short-cycle to full-degree programmes.

Make the offer more labour-market relevant

Recommendations

Several of the key challenges of the Finnish continuous learning provision relate to its relatively weak labour-market relevance. To ensure a provision that is responsive to the skill needs of the labour market, Finland could benefit from:

1. Systematising the use of skill anticipation information for strategic planning;
2. Harnessing the capacity of employers to develop training programmes;
3. Setting incentives for providers to offer training in line with skill demand.

Systematise the use of skill anticipation information for strategic planning.

Finnish stakeholders conduct a plethora of skill anticipation exercises, yet the mechanisms to translate this information into skill strategy and policy are underdeveloped. The planned parliamentary reform on continuous learning (Finnish Government, 2019[12]) should be used as a forum to review current practices in this area and develop systematic mechanisms by which skill anticipation informs the strategic planning of continuous learning policy. This could include the reinstatement of strategic plans in the area of continuous learning and institutionalising their regular update based on skill anticipation information. Any strategic plan will need to allow flexibility to adapt national level strategy to local labour market needs.

Many OECD economies are thinking about how to better link skill anticipation and strategic planning and it is difficult to point to one single country as an example of good practice across the board. Among countries that are already implementing the use of skills anticipation information in strategy planning the following stand out:

- Latvia has set a national strategic objective of increasing the share of students pursuing vocational upper secondary education to 50% by 2020 (compared to 39% in 2017/2018). The target is based on forecasts by the Ministry of Economics showing a shortage of workers with vocational degrees by 2025 (OECD, 2019[52]).
- In Estonia, annual reports on changes in labour market developments, labour requirements and the trends driving those changes are prepared under the OSKA skill anticipation system (OSKA, 2019[53]; OSKA, 2018[54]). The Estonian Unemployment Insurance Fund (Eesti Töötukassa) uses this information systematically to set training priorities in the context of active labour market policies.

Harness the capacity of employers to develop training programmes.

The role of employers in shaping the continuous learning provision in Finland is limited compared to their role in many other OECD economies and often primarily consultative, for example when anticipating skill needs or creating qualification requirements. Yet, employers have substantial knowledge on the skills needed in the labour market. Finland should harness the knowledge of employers to design labour-market relevant adult education and strengthen their involvement in the development of learning opportunities.

Employer involvement seems to already work relatively well at the local level, where employers develop training programmes in consultation with vocational or higher education providers. At the national level, the development of adult learning opportunities in Finland is strongly driven by public stakeholders, leaving limited space for more active involvement by employers. Other OECD countries give (groups of) employers stronger responsibility to shape training provision outside of governmental control and to share information about their training needs. In Ireland, for example, *Skillnet Ireland* is an agency that promotes and facilitates continuous learning in Ireland with the objective to increase learning participation in enterprises (Skillnet Ireland, 2019[55]). The agency supports more than 65 employer-led *Skillnet Learning Networks* representing specific sectors or regions throughout the country, which develop and deliver training. Networks are required to conduct a Learning Needs Assessment of their member enterprises to gather information about their skill development requirements. Skillnet Ireland operates a joint investment model, where government investment in on-the-job training (raised through training levys) is matched by contributions from businesses. In 2018, the networks delivered over EUR 36 million worth of education and training programmes to more than 56 000 individuals in Ireland. Currently, Skillnet Ireland has close to 16 500 member companies, 95% of which are small and medium enterprises and 56% are micro-enterprises with less than 10 employees (Skillnet Ireland, 2019[56]). Evaluations of Skillnet Ireland repeatedly show that companies perceive the training provided through the networks to be in line with labour market needs (Indecon, 2018[57]).

Iceland implements a different approach to involving employers in the development and implementation of adult learning. Its Education and Training Centre (*Fræðslumiðstöð atvinnulífsins*) is co-owned by the Confederation of Labour, the Confederation of Iceland Employers, the Federation of State and Municipal Employers, the Ministry of Finance and the Association of Local Authorities in Iceland. The Centre is contracted by the Ministry of Education, Science and Culture and has a wide range of responsibilities, including the identification of education needs, development and supervision of education and training programmes, development of training for adult educators, as well as administering the Education Fund. The Education Fund is funded through training levies and functions as funding vehicle for individual learning accounts in Iceland (OECD, 2019[58]; Education and Training Centre, n.d.[59]). The co-ownership of the centre through employer organisations is key to establish a true joint responsibility in the area of adult education and training.

Finland should consider how it can empower employers to more actively shape continuous learning provision at a national level. It should consider experimenting with employer-led approaches, for example in the development of labour-market relevant non-formal learning provision.

Incentivise providers to offer training in line with skill demand.

Funding for adult education and training providers is traditionally not tied to whether their training offer responds to the skill demands of the labour market or not. Some elements of 'effectiveness funding' have recently been introduced for vocational schools and universities, which induce mild incentives for adult learning provision to be more labour-market relevant. 15% of the funding for vocational education and training institutions will be based on indicators relating to graduates accessing employment or further studies following graduation (Ministry of Education and Culture/ Finnish National Agency for Education, 2018[60]). Along the same lines, 6% of funding for UAS and 4% of funding for Universities will be based on the number of employed graduates and the quality of their employment by 2021. Yet, the vast majority of funding continues to be dependent on the number of degrees awarded and student progression. It has been argued that such measures will have little impact on the alignment of the training offer with the skills need of the labour market, given that effectiveness funding is just a small share – and one of many – funding streams (OECD, 2017[9]).

Other OECD member economies use stronger incentives to steer adult learning provision in line with skill demand:

- **Variation of public funding depending on skill demand**: Denmark, for example, implements a *taximeter system* in the area of education funding. In the broadest sense, funding follows the users of education provision, which creates incentives for user-friendly behaviour. The grant is calculated based on the number of people participating in different education programmes, but the rates received per individual vary between programmes and groups of participants. Setting of rates is a political decision and takes into account societal and economic needs, as well as the costs and characteristics of a programme. Institutions are then free to use the obtained funding as they see fit, within existing frameworks (OECD, 2017[9]; Undervisningsministeriet, 2018[61]). Similarly, several Australian regions use skill anticipation information to determine the level of funding for vocational qualifications. In Queensland, for example, 'priority one' training courses for occupations in critical demand are 100% subsidised, while 'priority two and three' trainings are subsidised at a rate of 88 and 75% respectively (OECD, 2018[62]).
- **Regulating the set-up of new programmes**: Higher Vocational Education in Sweden (*Yrkeshögskolan*) aims to provide learning opportunities in line with labour market needs. Programmes have a typical duration of six months to two years. In the Swedish model, employers develop programme proposals together with education providers. They then back the funding application made to the Swedish National Agency for Higher Vocational Education. Funding can only be obtained when a programme proposal is employer backed and clearly outlines employer demand for the programme (OECD, 2017[9]; Tomaszewski, 2012[63]).

Finland should consider strengthening the link between the skill demands of the labour market and the funding of providers of continuous learning opportunities. Ensuring that the provision is in line with labour market needs is particularly relevant in Finland, as the options for steering individual choices for the take-up of provision are limited (see below).

Incentivise individuals to take part in the 'right' offer

> **Recommendations**
>
> Finland's tradition of public, universal and free adult learning provision has helped build motivation and raised participation. Yet, it yields an incentive structure that increasingly pushes adults to take-up formal learning opportunities, which may not be in line with their upskilling and reskilling needs. It also lacks incentives for adults to take-part in learning opportunities that equip them with the skills needed in the labour market. To steer educational choices of individuals, Finland could benefit from:
>
> 1. Providing better information on the labour-market relevance of training;
> 2. Reviewing and calibrating financial incentives for individuals.

Provide better information on the labour-market relevance of training.

Most adults in Finland take part in learning to improve their career prospects and progression. However, it is difficult for individuals to understand which skills are in demand in the labour market and to navigate the training offer in search of a programme where they can acquire these skills. Currently, individuals can find information about employment, education and training on various websites supported by different government departments and not all information is provided in a user-friendly way online (see e.g. https://opintopolku.fi/wp/fi/).

Developing virtual one-stop-shops with information on continuous learning opportunities is a key priority in many OECD Member economies. These one-stop-shops should ideally contain information on course availability, outcomes of course participants and their satisfaction, as well as more general information on skill and occupational labour market demand. Some countries are already operating successful websites that can be considered good practice:

- The Danish online Education Guide (*UddannelsenGuiden*, www.ug.dk) provides information on learning opportunities across educational levels. Further, it informs individuals about the structure of the labour market and current labour demand. Individuals can explore profiles of the most common occupations in Denmark. Individuals can obtain further information and guidance via chat, phone or email and contact details are clearly displayed.
- In the development of one-stop-shop websites, a balance has to be struck between providing comprehensive information and making the information easy to navigate for the users. The Icelandic website Next Steps (*Naesta skref*, naestaskref.is) presents information in a visually appealing and easily understandable format and includes videos, surveys and other visuals. The information provided is highly condensed with sign-posting to seek further information via email or in one of the Icelandic Lifelong Learning Centres. However, it does not include any information on labour market demand.
- Some countries have experimented with mobile apps to provide information on labour market prospects and training options. In New Zealand, the Occupation Outlook (occupationoutlook.mbie.govt.nz) is a mobile app that allows exploring study and career options, with extensive information on labour supply and demand in over 100 occupations.

Finnish stakeholders are aware of the fragmented nature of the available online information and are currently developing the Job-marketplace (*Työmarkkinatori*), a one-stop shop for continuous learning, employment opportunities and labour market information. Completion of the project is planned for 2020. Finland should ensure the swift development of the Job-marketplace, learn from international experience of providing such platforms, and test the platform extensively with different user groups.

It should also be noted that virtual information opportunities are typically not sufficient to help all adults make appropriate education and training choices. They should be accompanied by face-to-face advice and guidance services that offer holistic advice tailored to individual circumstances (see Chapter 4).

Review and calibrate financial incentives for individuals.

The public and universal nature of Finnish adult learning provision that comes at a low cost to the individual has many positives; not least, that it encourages high learning participation. Yet, it comes with the disadvantage that it does not take into account the private returns to training and may lead to deadweight losses and sub-optimal use of public resources.

More substantive forms of steering individual learning choices could take place through targeting existing financial support or exploring the introduction of new financial incentives. Incentives should be reviewed to introduce financial neutrality between formal and non-formal training options at the very least. Adjusting existing incentives to encourage the take-up of training towards skills in demand should be considered. Any system of financial incentives must be carefully calibrated and considered alongside other available benefits to prevent adverse effects.

Current financial incentives favour the take-up of formal education, which may not always be in line with individual training needs and which is more costly for society than shorter non-formal courses. This bias is both introduced through the free provision of formal education options (compared to many non-formal options) and the financial support for living expenses, available when taking part in formal education:

- In the future, Finland should continue to provide free access to formal higher and vocational education for adults who do not hold a degree at this level. To limit the number of people taking multiple successive degrees at the same level, a calibration of financial incentives should be explored. In Estonia, for example, individuals can pursue one tuition-free Bachelor's degree. Should they wish to obtain a different degree at the same level within a certain number of years of graduation, tuition fees are charged. Along the same lines, Hungary allows individuals to obtain a maximum of two vocational degrees free of charge.
- Eligibility criteria for existing financial support mechanisms should be reviewed: the Adult Education Allowance, Scholarships for Qualified Employees and funding for Self-Motivated Education supported by unemployment benefit are available for individuals pursuing full-time education leading to formal degrees or parts thereof (modules). Currently, only the Adjusted Adult Education Allowance can be used to fund non-formal adult education that enhances vocational expertise and competence. Austria, for example, faced similar challenges with its paid educational leave policy (*Bildungskarenz und Weiterbildungsgeld*). The policy has existed since 1998, but its use has been made more flexible over time, shortening the duration of courses eligible for funding and introducing funding for part-time education or training, both improving the possibilities of funding non-formal learning opportunities. The policy supports participation in formal and non-formal learning inside Austria and abroad, as long as it is job related. The job-relatedness of the learning opportunity is assessed on a case-by-case basis.

Further, Finland could consider linking some of the existing financial support mechanisms to the **take-up of training for skills in demand**. Many countries restrict financial support to programmes that provide skills in demand in the labour market:

- In Estonia, employed and unemployed individuals have access to the Degree Study Allowance (*Tasemeõppes osalemise toetus*) when they have trouble finding or keeping work due to insufficient or outdated education or skills. Eligible individuals include those who do not hold professional or vocational education, but have obtained a basic or general upper secondary degree more than five years ago; those who have obtained professional, vocational or higher education more than 15 years ago; and those who cannot continue in their current jobs due to health issues.

The allowance supports participation in selected state-commissioned training at vocational, professional higher or Bachelor's level. The selection of supported training is based on the OSKA skill anticipation system. Financial support is administered through the Estonian Public Employment Service (*Eesti Töötukassa*) and amounts to up to EUR 260 per month during the standard time it takes to complete the programme (Töötukassa, 2017[64]).

- Flanders (Belgium) has recently made its financial support for continuous learning more strongly dependent on labour-market relevance. From September 2019, private sector employees are eligible for 125 hours per year of Flemish training leave (*Vlaams opleidingsverlof, VOV*) (Flemish government, 2019[65]). Individuals are eligible for paid training leave if they take part in labour market or career oriented courses that meet certain conditions. Eligible courses are listed in the Flemish training database (*Opleidingsdatabank,* https://www.vlaanderen.be/opleidingsdatabank). During the leave, employees are entitled to receive their regular wage from their employer, up to EUR 2 928 gross per month. Employers are compensated for these costs with EUR 21.3 per hour of training leave. In the past, private sector employees were eligible for financial support of up to 180 hours per year. Eligibility was dependent on participation in officially recognised training and education programmes, although there was no criterion for labour-market relevance. Only the maximum number of 180 hours was reserved for those who took part in vocational training for shortage occupations or to obtain a first secondary education degree (OECD, 2019[66]).

- In Latvia, training vouchers have been available for unemployed individuals or those at risk of unemployment since 2011. Vouchers are administered by the public employment services and can be used to cover course costs of i) non-formal upskilling training programmes of 60-160 hours (voucher value: max. EUR 360); ii) advanced vocational training to reach vocational proficiency of 160 to 320 hours (voucher value: max. EUR 360); and iii) full vocational training programmes of 480 to 1280 hours (voucher value: max. EUR 1 100). Vouchers can only be used in priority training areas, which are specified by the Latvian Training Commission on a yearly basis. Priority training areas are identified based on skill anticipation information, including data from the PES, medium-term labour market forecasts, EU forecasts and recommendations, as well as recommendations from industry councils. (Ministry of Welfare of the Republic of Latvia, 2013[67]; OECD, 2019[68]; OECD, 2018[69])

In light of the examples above, Finland should explore the possibility of adjusting existing incentives to incentivise the take-up of labour-market relevant training. One potential adjustment of the Adult Education Allowance and the Scholarship for Qualified Employees could be to offer higher rates of financial support for those training towards skills or occupations in high demand. Another adjustment could be made to the funding for self-motivated education, by tying eligibility for the funding to training for skills or occupations in demand in the labour market or limiting it to adults who wish to upskill to a higher level than their initial studies.

References

Aittola, H. and J. Ursin (2019), "Finnish adult students' perspectives on short-cycle study programmes: motives and evaluations", *Higher Education Research and Development*, Vol. 38/2, pp. 205-218, http://dx.doi.org/10.1080/07294360.2018.1515182. [51]

Alatalo, J., L. Larja and E. Mähönen (2019), *Työ- ja elinkeinoministeriön lyhyen aikavälin työmarkkinaennuste, kevät 2019 [short-term labour market forecast for the Ministry of Employment and Economy]*, TEM, Helsinki, http://julkaisut.valtioneuvosto.fi/bitstream/handle/10024/161602/Ennuste%20kev%C3%A4t%202019_p%C3%A4ivitetty.pdf (accessed on 8 August 2019). [21]

Arnkill, R. (2010), *Anticipating and Managing Restructuring – Finland. National Background Paper.*, European Commission and ILO-ITC. [16]

Berge, T., L. Berg and S. Holm (2015), *Analysis, dialogue and dissemination of future skills needs A study of three countries*, https://www.kompetansenorge.no/contentassets/3d6da30c239940cd954ea144c5507839/anbalysis_dialogue_and_dissemination.pdf (accessed on 8 August 2019). [14]

BMAS (2019), *Die Bildungsprämie – Förderung für berufsbezogene Weiterbildung*, https://www.bildungspraemie.info/de/programm-bildungspraemie-21.php (accessed on 26 August 2019). [37]

Böckerman, P., M. Haapanen and C. Jepsen (2017), "More skilled, better paid: labour-market returns to postsecondary vocational education", *Oxford Economic Papers*, Vol. 70/2, pp. 485-508, http://dx.doi.org/10.1093/oep/gpx052. [34]

Bundesministerium für Justiz und Verbraucherschutz (2016), *Gesetz zur Förderung der beruflichen Aufstiegsfortbildung – Aufstiegsfortbildungsförderungsgesetz – (AFBG)*, https://www.aufstiegs-bafoeg.de/de/das-gesetz-im-wortlaut-1712.html (accessed on 26 August 2019). [41]

Bundesministerium für Justiz und Verbraucherschutz (2005), *Berufsbildungsgesetz (BBiG)*, https://www.gesetze-im-internet.de/bbig_2005/ (accessed on 26 August 2019). [42]

Bundesministeriums für Bildung, W. (2017), *Qualitätsrahmen für die Erwachsenenbildung in Österreich*, https://oe-cert.at/me- (accessed on 26 August 2019). [40]

Cremonini, L. (2010), *Short-Cycle Higher Education: An International Review*, https://www.wissenschaftsmanagement-online.de/sites/www.wissenschaftsmanagement-online.de/files/migrated_wimoarticle/001_CHEPS5ShortCycleHE.pdf (accessed on 27 August 2019). [46]

EAEA (2011), *Country Report on Adult Education in Flinland*, http://www.eaea.org/country/finland. [13]

Education and Training Centre (n.d.), *Fræðslumiðstöð atvinnulífsins | Menntun á vinnumarkaði*, 2019, https://frae.is/ (accessed on 28 August 2019). [59]

EPALE (2019), *Ö-Cert - an overall framework of quality for adult education in Austria*, EPALE, https://epale.ec.europa.eu/en/organisations/o-cert-overall-framework-quality-adult-education-austria-5 (accessed on 26 August 2019). [39]

Eurofound (2018), *Joint purchase training*, https://www.eurofound.europa.eu/observatories/emcc/erm/support-instrument/joint-purchase-training (accessed on 13 December 2018). [10]

Fazekas, M. and S. Field (2013), *A Skills beyond School Review of Switzerland*, OECD Reviews of Vocational Education and Training, OECD Publishing, Paris, https://dx.doi.org/10.1787/9789264062665-en. [43]

Fialho, P., G. Quintini and M. Vandeweyer (2019), "Returns to different forms of job related training: Factoring in informal learning", *OECD Social, Employment and Migration Working Papers*, No. 231, OECD Publishing, Paris, https://dx.doi.org/10.1787/b21807e9-en. [32]

Finnish Board of Education (2019), *Osaaminen 2035 - Osaamisen ennakointifoorumin ensimmäisiä ennakointituloksia [Expertise 2035 - First Foresight Results from the Foresight Forum]*, Finnish Board of Education, Helsinki, http://www.oph.fi. [20]

Finnish Government (2019), *Inclusive and competent Finland - a socially, economically and ecologically sustainable society*, Publication of the Finnish Government, Helsinki, http://julkaisut.valtioneuvosto.fi/bitstream/handle/10024/161664/Inclusive%20and%20competent%20Finland_2019.pdf?sequence=7&isAllowed=y (accessed on 8 July 2019). [12]

Finnish National Agency for Education (2018), *Report on the referencing of the Finnish National Qualifications Framework to the European Qualifications Framework and the Framework for Qualifications of the European Higher Education Area*, Finnish National Agency for Education/ Ministry of Education and Culture, Helsinki, http://www.oph.fi/qualificationsframework (accessed on 2 August 2019). [1]

Finnish National Agency for Education (2017), *The anticipation plan of the National Forum for Skills Anticipation*. [19]

Finnish National Agency of Education (2019), *Work life changes - how does education respond? Proposals published by the Knowledge Forecasting Forum Board of Education*, https://www.oph.fi/fi/uutiset/2019/tyoelama-muuttuu-miten-koulutus-vastaa-osaamisen-ennakointifoorumi-julkisti (accessed on 9 August 2019). [28]

Flemish government (2019), *Vlaams opleidingsverlof (VOV)*, https://www.vlaanderen.be/vlaams-opleidingsverlof-vov (accessed on 29 August 2019). [65]

Hanhijoki, I. et al. (2012), *Education, training and demand for labour in Finland by 2025*, Finnish National Board of Education, http://www.oph.fi (accessed on 5 March 2019). [27]

Headai (2019), *Customer Story: Helsinki Metropolitan Universities of Applied Sciences*, Medium, https://medium.com/headai-customer-stories/customer-story-3amk-4f7944080344 (accessed on 10 September 2019). [24]

Honkatukia, J. (2009), *VATTAGE-A dynamic, applied general equilibrium model of the Finnish economy*, Government Institute for Economic Research, Helsinki, https://www.doria.fi/bitstream/handle/10024/148683/t150.pdf?sequence=1&isAllowed=y (accessed on 8 August 2019). [18]

Indecon (2018), *Evaluation of Skillnet Ireland in 2017*, http://www.indecon.ie (accessed on 28 August 2019). [57]

JAMK (2019), *Diploma of Higher Education*, https://www.jamk.fi/en/Education/Open-studies/diploma-of-higher-education/ (accessed on 27 August 2019). [50]

Jauhiainen, A., H. Nori and M. Alho-Malmelin (2007), "Various Portraits of Finnish Open University Students", *Scandinavian Journal of Educational Research*, Vol. 51/1, pp. 23-39, http://dx.doi.org/10.1080/00313830601079017. [5]

Kaivo-Oja, J. and J. Marttinen (2008), *Foresight systems and core activities at national and regional levels in Finland 1990-2008 Developing Foresight Systems for a Better Life in Finland and Europe*, Finland Futures Research Centre. Turku School of Economics, Turku, https://www.utu.fi/fi/yksikot/ffrc/julkaisut/e-tutu/Documents/eTutu_2008-6.pdf (accessed on 9 August 2019). [31]

Kauhanen, A. (2018), "The Effects of an Education-Leave Program on Educational Attainment and Labor-Market Outcomes", *ETLA Working Papers*, http://pub.etla.fi/ETLA-Working-Papers-56.pdf. [33]

Ketamo, H. et al. (2019), *Mapping the Future Curriculum: Adopting Artifical Intelligence and Analytics in Forecasting Competence Needs.*, http://urn.fi/URN:NBN:fi-fe2019053117966 (accessed on 10 September 2019). [23]

Kirsch, M. and Y. Beernaert (2011), *Short Cycle Higher Education in Europe. Level 5: the Missing Link*, EURASHE, Brussels, http://www.eurashe.eu/library/modernising-phe/L5_report_SCHE_in_Europe_full_report_Jan2011.pdf (accessed on 26 August 2019). [45]

Kumpulainen, T. (2016), *Key figures on apprenticeship training in Finland*, Finnish National Board of Education, Helsinki. [3]

Leetma, R. et al. (2015), *Counterfactual Impact Evaluation (CIE) of Estonian Adult Vocational Training Activity*, Praxis, Tallinn, http://www.praxis.ee (accessed on 7 July 2019). [36]

Ministry of Education and Culture (2019), *Higher education and degrees*, https://minedu.fi/en/higher-education-and-degrees (accessed on 2 August 2019). [4]

Ministry of Education and Culture (2019), "Jatkuvan oppimisen kehittäminen - työryhmän väliraportti [Developing continuous learning - working party report]", Ministry of Education and Culture, Helsinki. [35]

Ministry of Education and Culture (2019), *Qualifications and studies in vocational training*, https://minedu.fi/en/qualifications-and-studies_vet (accessed on 2 August 2019). [2]

Ministry of Education and Culture/ Finnish National Agency for Education (2018), *Finnish VET in a Nutshell*, Ministry of Education and Culture, Helsinki, https://minedu.fi/documents/1410845/4150027/Finnish+VET+in+a+Nutshell.pdf/9d43da93-7b69-d4b5-f939-93a541ae9980/Finnish+VET+in+a+Nutshell.pdf.pdf (accessed on 28 August 2019). [60]

Ministry of Labour (2007), *Laki yhteistoiminnasta yrityksissä [Act on Collaboration in Enterprises*, Oikeusministeriö, Helsinki, https://www.finlex.fi/fi/laki/smur/2007/20070334 (accessed on 6 September 2019). [7]

Ministry of the Interior (2007), *Laki työnantajan ja henkilöstön välisestä yhteistoiminnasta kunnissa [Act on Cooperation between Employers and Employees in Municipalities]*, Oikeusministeriö, Edita Publishing Oy, https://www.finlex.fi/fi/laki/smur/2007/20070449 (accessed on 6 September 2019). [8]

Ministry of Welfare of the Republic of Latvia (2013), *Training Voucher System in Latvia*. [67]

Nyyssölä, K. (2019), *The Finnish Anticipation System*, Finnish National Agency of Education, Helsinki. [17]

OECD (2019), *Evaluating Latvia's Active Labour Market Policies*, Connecting People with Jobs, OECD Publishing, Paris, https://dx.doi.org/10.1787/6037200a-en. [68]

OECD (2019), *Getting Skills Right: Creating responsive adult learning systems*, OECD, Paris, http://www.oecd.org/els/emp/adult-learning-systems-2019.pdf. [11]

OECD (2019), *Getting Skills Right: Future-Ready Adult Learning Systems*, Getting Skills Right, OECD Publishing, Paris, https://dx.doi.org/10.1787/9789264311756-en. [58]

OECD (2019), *Individual Learning Accounts : Panacea or Pandora's Box?*, OECD Publishing, Paris, https://dx.doi.org/10.1787/203b21a8-en. [38]

OECD (2019), *OECD Skills Strategy Flanders*, OECD Publishing, Paris, https://doi.org/10.1787/9789264309791-en. [66]

OECD (2019), *OECD Skills Strategy Latvia: Assessment and Recommendations*, OECD Skills Studies, OECD Publishing, Paris, https://dx.doi.org/10.1787/74fe3bf8-en. [52]

OECD (2018), *Country note United Kingdom. Education at a glance*, OECD Publishing, Paris, http://gpseducation.oecd.org/Content/EAGCountryNotes/GBR.pdf (accessed on 27 August 2019). [49]

OECD (2018), *Denmark-Country Note -Education at a Glance*, http://gpseducation.oecd.org/Content/EAGCountryNotes/DNK.pdf (accessed on 27 August 2019). [47]

OECD (2018), *Getting Skills Right: Australia*, Getting Skills Right, OECD Publishing, Paris, https://dx.doi.org/10.1787/9789264303539-en. [62]

OECD (2018), *Inclusive Entrepreneurship Policies: Country Assessment Notes - Latvia*, OECD, Paris, http://www.oecd.org/employment/leed/inclusive-entrepreneurship.htm. (accessed on 29 August 2019). [69]

OECD (2017), *Financial Incentives for Steering Education and Training*, Getting Skills Right, OECD Publishing, Paris, https://dx.doi.org/10.1787/9789264272415-en. [9]

OECD (2016), *Back to Work: Finland: Improving the Re-employment Prospects of Displaced Workers*, Back to Work, OECD Publishing, Paris, https://dx.doi.org/10.1787/9789264264717-en. [15]

OECD (2015), "ISCED 2011 Level 5: Short-cycle tertiary education", in *ISCED 2011 Operational Manual: Guidelines for Classifying National Education Programmes and Related Qualifications*, OECD Publishing, Paris, https://dx.doi.org/10.1787/9789264228368-10-en. [48]

OECD (2003), *Reviews of National Policies for Education: Polytechnic Education in Finland 2003*, Reviews of National Policies for Education, OECD Publishing, Paris, https://dx.doi.org/10.1787/9789264199408-en. [29]

OECD (2001), *Thematic Review on Adult Learning. Finland. Country note.*, OECD, Paris, https://www.oecd.org/education/skills-beyond-school/2541579.pdf (accessed on 8 May 2019). [6]

OECD (1999), *Thematic Review of the Transition From Initial Education to Working Life*, OECD Publishing, Paris, http://www.oecd.org/edu/skills-beyond-school/1908252.pdf (accessed on 6 August 2019). [30]

OSKA (2019), *Estonian labor market today and tomorrow*, https://oska.kutsekoda.ee/tulevikutrendid/eesti-tooturg-tana-ja-homme/ (accessed on 27 August 2019). [53]

OSKA (2018), *Eesti tööturg täna ja homme [Estonian labour market today and tomorrow]*, https://oska.kutsekoda.ee/wp-content/uploads/2018/12/Eesti-t%c3%b6%c3%b6turg-t%c3%a4na-ja-homme-2018.pdf (accessed on 27 August 2019). [54]

Sitra (2019), *How can we predict what expertise will be needed in the future? Artificial intelligence knows - Sitra*, https://www.sitra.fi/en/articles/can-predict-expertise-will-needed-future-artificial-intelligence-knows/ (accessed on 10 September 2019). [25]

Sitra (2017), *Artificial intelligence shows what Finland can do and a positive CV reveals the hidden talents of young people: The winners of Sitra's million-euro Ratkaisu 100 Challenge competition*, https://www.sitra.fi/en/news/artificial-intelligence-shows-finland-can-positive-cv-reveals-hidden-talents-young-people-winners-sitras-100-million-euro-ratkaisu-100-challenge-competition/ (accessed on 10 September 2019). [26]

Skillnet Ireland (2019), *Developing the workforce of Ireland through enterprise led learning. Annual report 2018*, https://www.skillnetireland.ie/wp-content/uploads/2019/07/Skillnet-Ireland-Annual-Report-2018.pdf (accessed on 28 August 2019). [56]

Skillnet Ireland (2019), *Skillnet Ireland | The National Agency for Workforce Learning*, https://www.skillnetireland.ie/ (accessed on 28 August 2019). [55]

Skills Panorama (2017), "Skills anticipation in Finland", *Analytical highlights series*, https://skillspanorama.cedefop.europa.eu/en/analytical_highlights/skills-anticipation-finland (accessed on 8 August 2019). [22]

Staatssekretariat für Bildung, F. (2017), *Berufsbildung in der Schweiz*, SBFI, Bern. [44]

Tomaszewski, R. (2012), *The Swedish Model of Higher Vocational Education*. [63]

Töötukassa (2017), *Degree study allowance*, https://www.tootukassa.ee/eng/content/prevention-unemployment/degree-study-allowance (accessed on 29 August 2019). [64]

Undervisningsministeriet (2018), *The taximeter system*. [61]

Notes

[1] An exception is the IVET qualification of Air Traffic Controller, which is referenced at level 5 of FinQF due to more stringent skill requirements.

[2] 84% participate for job-related reasons according to OECD PIAAC data.

[3] https://www.ammattibarometri.fi.

[4] Agricultural Entrepreneur Business Competences, Gerontological Rehabilitation, HR and Financial Specialists, and Purchasing Professionals.

4 Improving learning participation of adults with low skills

More than one in ten adults in Finland have low basic skills. Employment opportunities for this group have shrunk over the past decades, highlighting the need to upskill for an increasingly knowledge-driven economy. However, Finnish adults with low basic skills are half as likely to train as those with higher skill levels. There is an urgent need to review where the current adult learning system falls short in engaging low-skilled adults and find targeted solutions for this group. This chapter first provides an overview of adults with low skills in Finland, their training participation patterns and the learning provision available to them. It then highlights the key reasons behind low participation, challenges for engaging the group in learning and outlines possible policy responses.

Introduction

Finland has the largest participation gap between adults with low basic skills and those with higher skill levels amongst all OECD economies. This is of concern as the employment opportunities for low-skilled adults are shrinking. According to data from the Ministry of Economic Affairs and Employment, two-thirds of new job opportunities in the past five years were generated in high skilled occupations. At an individual level, the lack of engagement in upskilling or reskilling decreases the employability of adults with low skills by putting them at risk of job loss or limiting their chances of finding employment. It can therefore lower their incomes and well-being. This also has implications for the economy as a whole, including lower tax revenues, higher benefit expenditure, decreased productivity, slower technology adoption and consequently decreased competitiveness (Woessmann, 2016[1]).

Supporting adults with low skills to upskill or reskill is therefore an economic imperative for a future of work that is more inclusive and productive. Barriers to accessing learning provision are already low in Finland, with much of the provision being offered for free or at a low-cost to the individual, delivered flexibly and in principle being open to adults at all skill levels, raising the question of what more can be done to engage adults with low skills in learning. This chapter discusses where the challenges lie in engaging adults with low skills in Finland, including a lack of outreach activities, targeted and comprehensive information, and guidance services, as well as the need for specific training provision for this target group. It makes recommendations on how to tackle these issues drawing on international good practices.

In this chapter, all data refers to adults with low basic skills. When this is not available, data on adults with low qualifications are used (for definitions see Box 4.1). Key challenges and recommendations are equally valid for both groups.

Box 4.1. Defining adults with low skills

There are many different ways to define adults with low skills. In this report, **adults with low basic skills** refer to individuals with low proficiency in literacy, numeracy or both. For the purpose of international comparisons, OECD PIAAC data are used where adults with low skills are defined as those aged 25-64 who scored at Level 1 or below on the literacy or numeracy dimensions of the assessment. These are adults, who at most understand brief texts on familiar topics and/or are able to do simple mathematical processing such as one-step calculations or simple percentages.

Adults with low qualification levels (aged 25-64) are those whose highest educational attainment level is at most lower secondary education (ISCED 0-2). In the Finnish context, these adults have left education after compulsory comprehensive school or earlier. Given the importance of qualifications in the Finnish labour market, having low qualifications puts individuals in a vulnerable position.

The group of adults with low basic skills and those with low qualifications are not identical, but overlap. For instance, some adults with low qualifications may actually have good levels of basic skills. By contrast, some adults with higher qualifications may have low levels of basic skills, because of skill depreciation or poor quality of their initial education. Irrespective, both low-qualified and low-skilled adults are strongly exposed to the consequences of changing demand for skills in the labour market, increasing the need for them to upskill or reskill to stay in employment.

Source: Musset, (2015[2]), "Building Skills For All: A Review of Finland. Policy Insights on literacy, numeracy and digital skills from the survey of adult skills", http://www.oecd.org/finland/Building-Skills-For-All-A-Review-of-Finland.pdf; OECD (2019[3]), "Getting Skills Right: Engaging low-skilled adults in learning", http://www.oecd.org/employment/emp/engaging-low-skilled-adults-2019.pdf.

The current situation

To improve the engagement of low-skilled adults it is essential to analyse their participation patterns and understand who they are, what kind of learning they already participate in, their reasons for non-participation and what education provision is available to them.

Profile of adults with low basic skills in Finland

Finland has one of the lowest shares of adults with low basic skills across OECD economies, second only to Japan. Around 12% of the 25-64 year old population have low literacy, low numeracy skills or both (Figure 4.1).These are adults who can at most complete very simple reading tasks, such as reading brief texts on familiar topics, or mathematical tasks, such as simple processes involving counting, sorting, basic arithmetic operations and understanding simple percentages (OECD, 2019[3]). Low basic skills in literacy and numeracy tend to go together: 7% of adults score low in both dimensions in the PIAAC survey (i.e. nearly 60% of the low-skilled adult population), while 3% display low basic numeracy and 2% low basic literacy only.

Figure 4.1. The share of adults with low basic skills is comparatively small in Finland

Adults age 25-64 with low basic skills in literacy and/or numeracy, 2012/2015, %

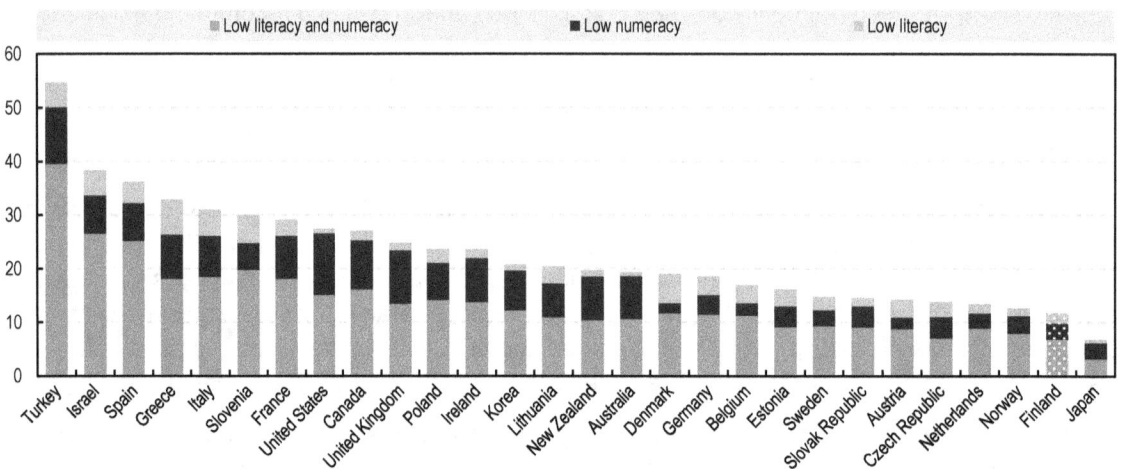

Note: Low-skilled refers to adults scoring at level 1 or below in literacy and/or numeracy in PIAAC. Belgium refers to Flanders, United Kingdom refers to England and Northern Ireland only.
Source: PIAAC (2012, 2015).

Socio-demographic background

Who are these adults with low basic skills? First, it is important to note that a low level of basic skills does not automatically mean that an individual also has weak occupational skills, or low qualifications. Only around one-third of Finnish adults with low skills have low qualifications; half of them hold an upper-secondary qualification, while more than one in ten holds a tertiary qualification (

These shares are higher than in other Nordic countries. As numeracy and literacy are becoming increasingly important for carrying out work and for continuous learning; many of these individuals may not be able cope with the ongoing changes in the labour market despite their higher qualification levels (Musset, 2015[2]). Looking at demographic variables (Figure 4.2), adults with low basic skills are more likely to be older and/or a non-native Finnish speaker than adults with higher level skills. More than half of adults with low basic skills are above the age of 55 and hence likely to have completed school before the fundamental reform of the initial education system in the 1970s (Pareliussen, 2016[4]). The gender composition of the group is relatively balanced (more so than in other countries), the share of low-skilled men is only slightly higher than the share of low-skilled women. Some 44% of those with migrant background have low basic skills (or at least when tested in Finnish) and they make up 13% of all adults with low basic skills. The strong impact of migrant status, language background and age on proficiency in basic skills is confirmed by a large body of research (see e.g. Flisi et al (2018[5]), OECD (2018[6]), Sulkunen and Malin (2018[7])). This highlights the importance of providing language and basic skills training to immigrants as well as up-skilling opportunities for older adults.

Socio-economic background is strongly associated with skill levels in Finland; the strongest association across all Nordic countries (Norden, 2015[8]). Around 70% of adults with low basic skills have parents who hold at most lower secondary qualifications, compared to 57% of adults with low basic skills in other Nordic countries (Figure 4.2). The impact of parental background on skill levels has increased over time and is more pronounced in younger cohorts (Musset, 2015[2]). This may point to systemic issues related to social mobility.

Adults with low level of basic skills also earn less on average than their higher skilled counterparts. 18% of them earn at most two third of the national median wage (considered low income), which is slightly higher than in other Nordic countries (Figure 4.2). This makes training costs and forgone wages a more important barrier for them, underlining the importance of financial support for both direct and indirect costs of training when targeting this group.

Figure 4.2. Adults with low basic skills are typically older, from low socio-economic background and/or migrants

Adults age 25-64 with selected characteristics by skill level, Finland and other Nordic countries, 2012, %

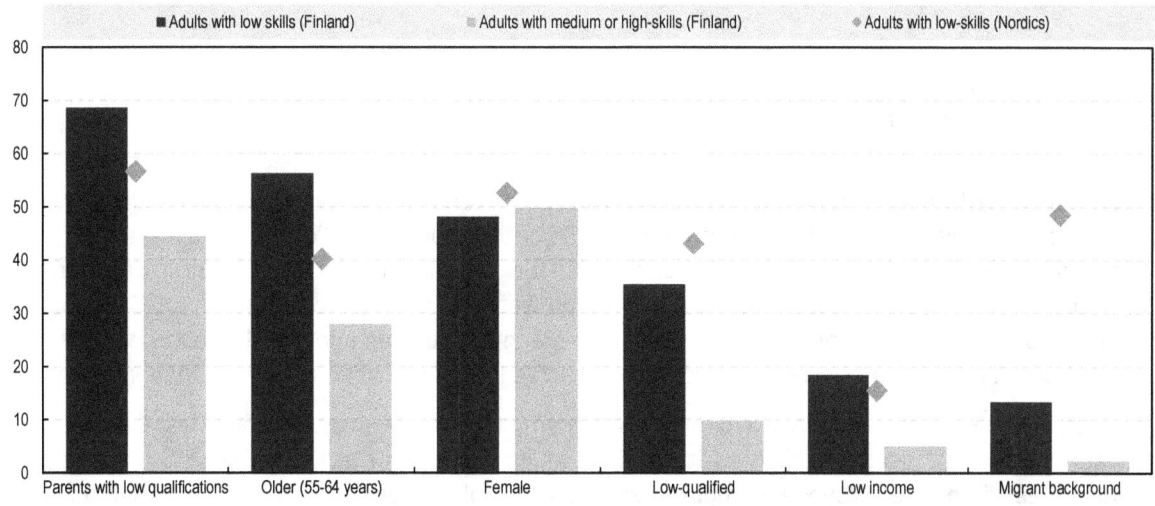

Note: Low-skilled refers to adults scoring at level 1 or below in literacy and/or numeracy in PIAAC; parents with low qualifications refers to neither parent having attained upper secondary or post-secondary education; low-qualified refers to at most holding a ISCED Level 0 2 qualification; low income relates to earnings that are at most two thirds of the national median wage; migrant background refers to being a first and second generation immigrant; Nordic countries refer to Denmark, Norway and Sweden without Finland. The low-income variable is expressed as share in the employed population.
Source: PIAAC (2012).

Labour market situation

The majority of adults with low qualifications in Finland are employed (53%), while 8% are unemployed and 39% are inactive (Figure 4.3). Adults with low skills are less likely to have a job than their higher skilled counterparts: only 53% for adults with lower secondary educational attainment are employed compared with 73% for those with upper secondary qualifications, and 86% for those with tertiary qualifications. This employment gap across qualification levels is relatively high compared with other Nordic countries. However, the incidence of temporary work for Finnish adults with low qualifications is similar to that for those with medium or high skills (11% and 12% respectively).

Figure 4.3. A high share of adults with low skills are inactive

Low qualified adults age 20-64 by employment status, 2018, %

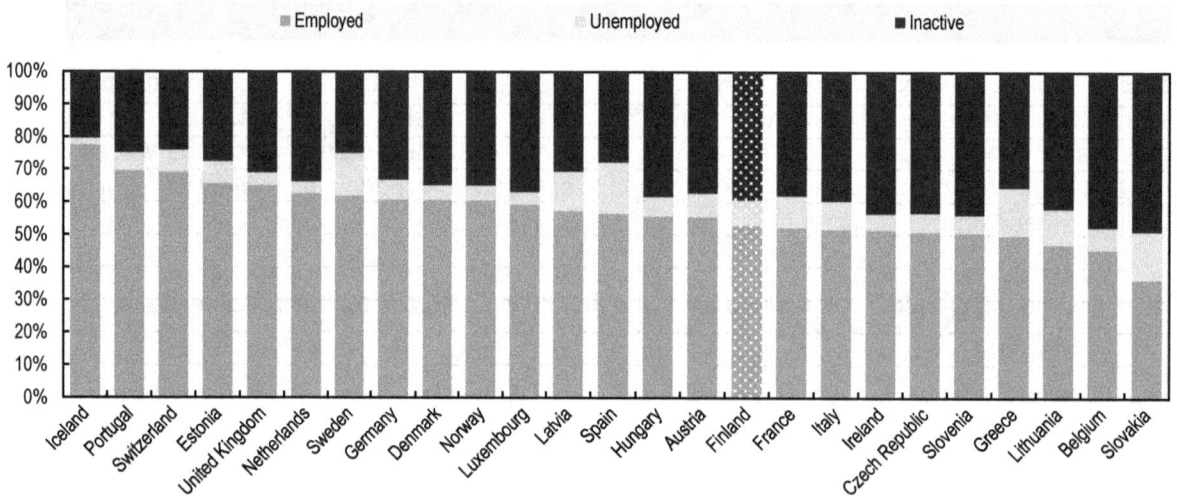

Note: Low-skilled refers to adults scoring at level 1 or below in literacy and/or numeracy in PIAAC.
Source: Labour Force Survey (2018).

Compared to other Nordic countries or the OECD average, a considerably larger share of adults with low basic skills are inactive. PIAAC data confirms that 27% of them are retired or on early retirement, while 10% are out of work due to a permanent disability. However, inactivity due to caring and domestic responsibilities is relatively low; less than 2% compared with 4% in Nordic and 14% in OECD countries. This highlights the importance of taking health and mental health issues into consideration and the need to provide complex services in order to overcome obstacles in the way of training participation.

Adults with low basic skills in Finland typically work in smaller, private sector companies. Only 28% are employed in the public sector, compared to 34% of adults with higher skills, while 36% work at micro enterprises (less than 10 employees) compared with 25% of higher skilled adults. Self-employment is also more frequent amongst adults with low basic skills (16% vs. 12% respectively) (Figure 4.4) and, according to Labour Force Survey data, this share has increased over time. Therefore, to reach adults with low basic skills, policies should pay special attention to workers in micro, small and medium enterprises and entrepreneurs.

Figure 4.4. Adults with low level of basic skills tend to work at smaller private sector companies

Employed adults age 25-64 with selected characteristics by skill level, Finland and other Nordic countries, 2012, %

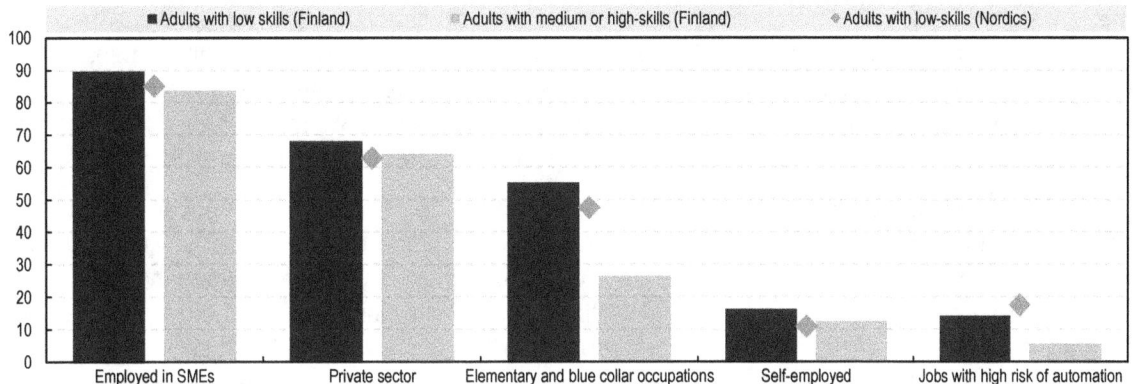

Note: Low-skilled refers to adults scoring at level 1 or below in literacy and/or numeracy in PIAAC. Nordic countries refer to Denmark, Norway and Sweden without Finland. SMEs refer to small and medium enterprises (below 250 employees). Jobs with high risk of automation are jobs where more than 70% of the tasks performed are automatable.
Source: PIAAC (2012).

Adults with low basic skills in Finland are over-represented in agriculture, manufacturing, construction and some of the services industries (transportation and storage or accommodation and food), which feature more manual and routine jobs. They are underrepresented in public services, in particular in the areas of education and public administration (Figure 4.5). Additionally, more than half of this group works in lower level occupations (blue collar or elementary occupations) compared with only a quarter of adults with higher-level basic skills. It is therefore not surprising that their job's risk of automation is close to three times higher than that of adults with higher-level skills (14% and 5% respectively). This highlights the need for upskilling and reskilling of this target group to ensure their employability in the future.

Figure 4.5. Low-skilled adults are overrepresented in sectors with more manual and routine jobs

Adults age 25-64 working in different sectors by skill level, Finland, %

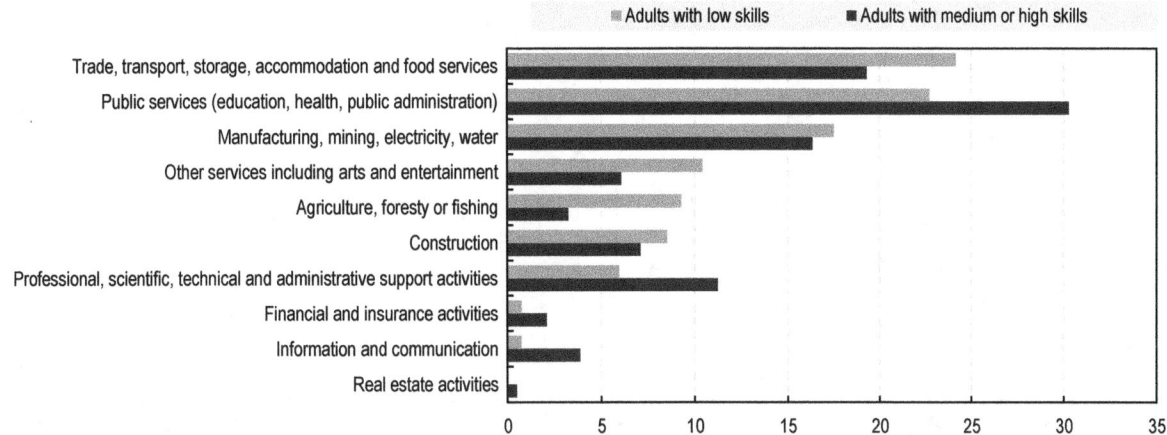

Note: Low-skilled refers to adults scoring at level 1 or below in literacy and/or numeracy in PIAAC. Industry categories are created by grouping the respective ISIC categories.
Source: PIAAC (2012).

Box 4.2. Profile of adults with low educational attainment compared to those with low basic skills

Adults with low educational attainment make up 11% of the Finnish population, a similarly large share as the low skilled (12%). Their characteristics are also very similar with a few exceptions. Based on PIAAC data, a higher share of adults with low educational attainment tend to be older men, whose parents only have low education attainment. The most striking difference is the low share of immigrants among adults with low qualifications, which is only 5% compared with 13% for the share of adults with low basic skills. This is not significantly larger than the share of migrants in the general population (3%).

Employed adults with low educational attainment are even more concentrated in the private sector, blue collar or elementary jobs. In line with this, an even higher share of this group have jobs with a high risk of automation than adults with low basic skills (18% vs 14%). A main difference between the two groups is employment in public-services (education, health and public administration), where an even lower share, only 8% of low-qualified adults work compared to 23% of those with low basic skills. This is likely due to qualification playing a bigger role in the public sector as an entry requirement. According to LFS data, the employment rate of adults with low educational attainment decreased over the past decades, especially among the younger cohorts, which further signals the importance/need of upskilling.

Learning participation of adults with low basic skills

At 31%, job-related learning participation of adults with low basic skills is relatively high in Finland by international standards. However, it lags behind participation in the Nordic neighbour economies Denmark (33%), Norway (40%) and Sweden (32%). Furthermore, at 31 percentage points, the participation gap between adults with low basic skills and their higher skilled counterparts is the largest across OECD economies (Figure 4.6). Looking at differences across types of learning (formal, non-formal, and informal), it emerges that the difference is the largest in the area of formal education. Given the low participation of adults with low basic skills, the current continuous learning system further widens the skill gap that exists at the end of initial education.

Figure 4.6. Participation gap between low and medium/high skilled adults is largest in the OECD

Adults aged 25-64 who participated in job-related education and training in the past 12 months, 2012/2015, %

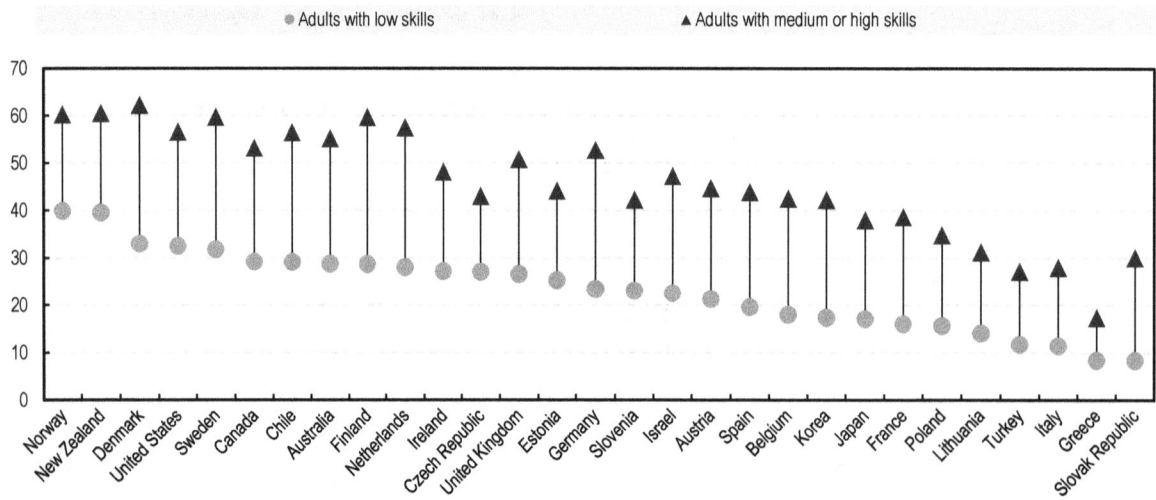

Note: Participation in formal or non-formal adult education. Low-skilled refers to adults scoring at level 1 or below in literacy and/or numeracy in PIAAC. Belgium refers to Flanders, United Kingdom refers to England and Northern Ireland.
Source: PIAAC (2012, 2015).

Of the large share of adults with low basic skills who do not participate in training, one in six people were willing to participate in training, but did not for various reasons (Figure 4.7). The share of those willing but unable to train is lower than in other Nordic countries, suggesting that barriers for those interested in education and training are relatively low. However, it should be noted that the share of those who neither take part in education and training nor are willing to take part – 61% of all adults with low basic skills – is much higher than in Denmark (55%), Norway (50%) and Sweden (50%).

Figure 4.7. Many adults with low skills neither participate nor do they want to

Adults aged 25-64 with low skills who participated in job-related education and training in the past 12 months, 2012/2015, %

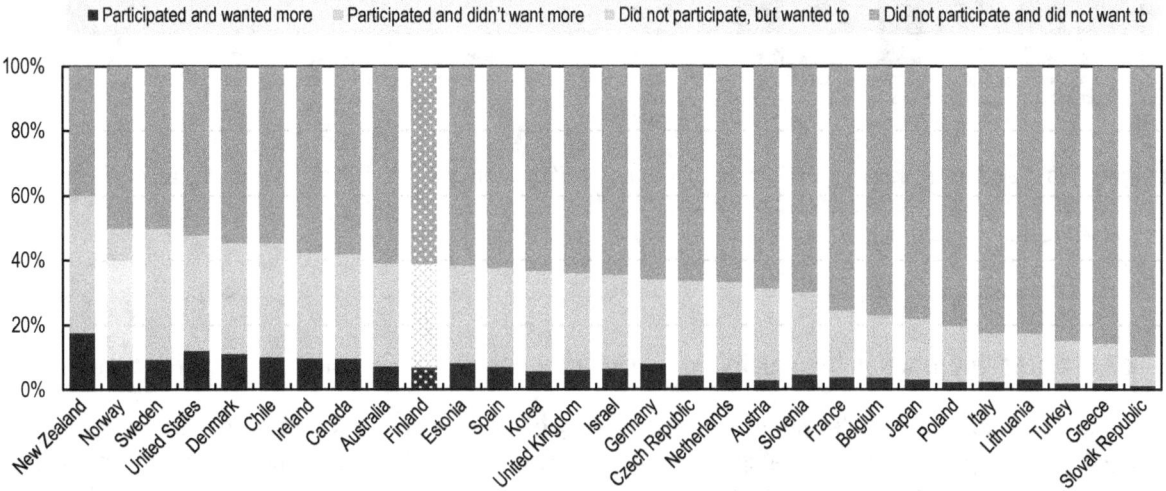

Note: Participation in formal or non-formal job related adult education. Low-skilled refers to adults scoring at level 1 or below in literacy and/or numeracy in PIAAC. Belgium refers to Flanders, United Kingdom refers to England and Northern Ireland.
Source: PIAAC (2012, 2015).

While learning participation is lower, adults with low basic skills tend to take part in longer non-formal education and training programmes compared with higher skilled adults. When they participate they do so for an average of four weeks per year (154 hours), which is close to double the time spent in non-formal education by their medium/higher skilled counterparts, according to PIAAC data. At the same time, job-related learning makes up a smaller share of their training time: 43% compared to 75% of adults with medium/high skill levels.

Reasons for participation in learning

The top three reasons for participating in learning are the same for adults with low basic skills or with higher levels of basic skills. Yet, there are some differences: adults with low basic skills are less likely to participate in learning to increase their knowledge and skills in a topic of interest or to do their job better. They are more likely to participate because they are obliged or out of fear of losing their job (Figure 4.8). These differences highlight a lower engagement of adults with low basic skills in learning, which must be taken into account when designing programmes or services for them.

Figure 4.8. Many adults with low basic skills participate in learning because they have to

Main reason for participating in learning by skill level, Finland, %

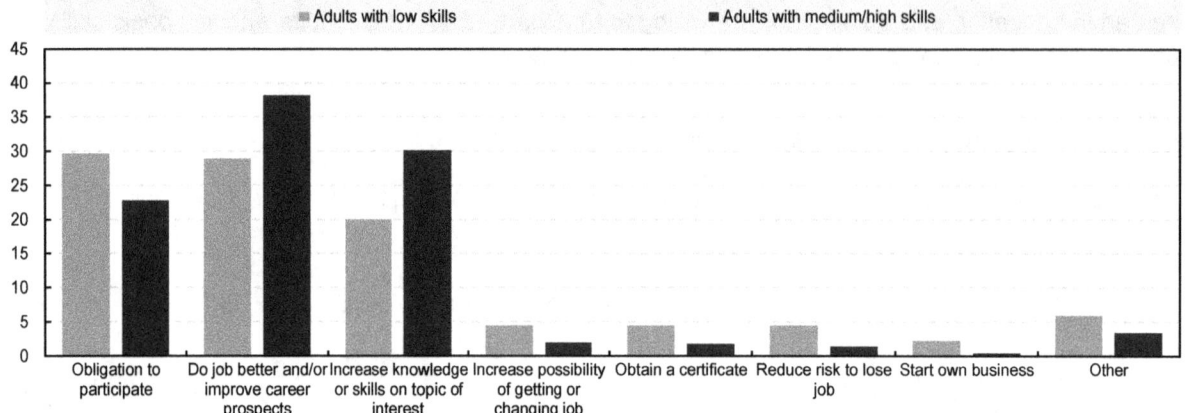

Note: Low-skilled refers to adults scoring at level 1 or below in literacy and/or numeracy in PIAAC. Reasons for participation in formal or non-formal adult education for job-related reasons in past 12 months.
Source: PIAAC (2012).

Box 4.3. Some approaches to explain the low willingness to train among adults with low skills

It is a key question why adults with low skills so rarely take up learning opportunities. Barriers to adult education participation can be categorised into structural (e.g. lack of appropriate opportunities), physical or material (e.g. costs, time or information) and attitudinal barriers (e.g. lack of motivation) (Hillage and Aston, 2001[9]). The academic literature provides the following explanations for attitudinal barriers, i.e. the lower willingness of adults with low basic skills to train:

- **Undervaluing the benefits and overvaluing the costs of education:** They may underestimate the potential increase in earnings, overvalue the costs of studying (e.g. cognitive effort, fees, forgone earnings) or discount the future too much. This leads to lower perceived returns to education. They also tend to disregard indirect benefits of additional education such as wider networks, and an improved ability to take care of their own health, cope with changes and manage risks. (Lavecchia, Liu and Oreopoulos, 2015[10])

- **Negative experiences encountered in initial education:** Experiences such as failing in a subject or feeling inferior to classmates can stick with individuals even in adulthood building up a fear of learning. This lowers individuals' confidence in their own abilities to perform well in an academic context, which is strongly correlated with worse educational outcomes and lower persistence in education (Semmar, 2006[11]). Negative attitudes and low motivation are strongest towards formal and classroom-based education, but can even spill over to informal opportunities specifically designed for them.

- **Group dynamics or network effect:** They are typically surrounded by other adults with similar skill levels and with similar attitudes towards education and training. This can have a negative effect on their training choices and further contribute to low willingness to participate (Veronica McGivney, 1993[12]). By contrast, knowing someone who participated in adult learning increases one's self-efficacy and willingness to participate (Goto and Martin, 2009[13]).

Learning participation of workers with low basic skills

When in employment, adults with low basic skills in Finland participate more in education and training and the gap with the higher skilled is lower (22 percentage points). Moreover, their participation is very similar to that observed in Denmark and even slightly higher than in Sweden (Figure 4.9).

Figure 4.9. The participation rate of low-skilled employed adults in Finland is comparatively high

Employed adults age 25-64 who participated in job-related education and training, by skill level, %

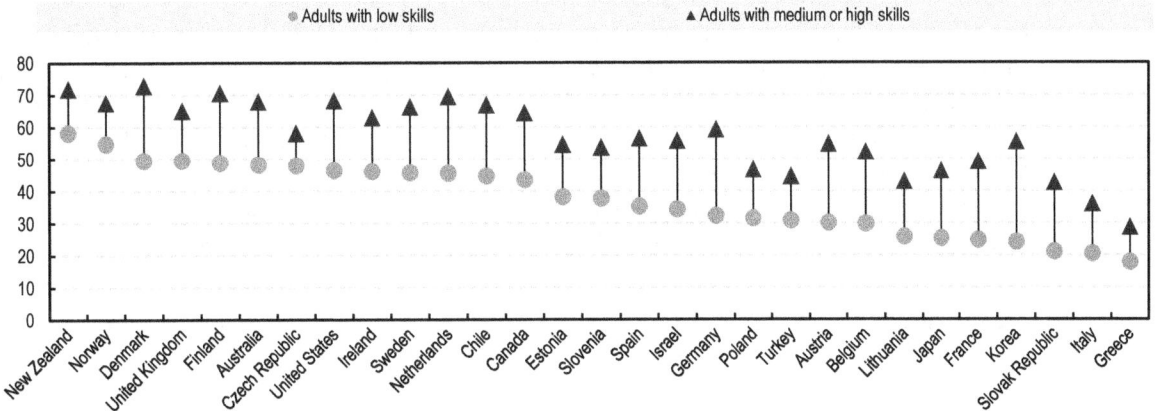

Note: Adults in dependent employment, excluding self-employed; formal or non-formal adult education; low-skilled defined as adults scoring at level 1 or below in literacy and/or numeracy in PIAAC; Belgium refers to Flanders, United Kingdom to England and Northern Ireland.
Source: PIAAC (2012, 2015).

One of the reasons for the relatively high participation of workers with low skills in Finland may be that they benefit from comparatively strong financial support from employers for training. According to PIAAC data, 89% of adult learners with low basic skills state that they have their employers pay their course fees in full. This is a considerably higher share than in Norway (78%) or Sweden (81%). Meanwhile the gap between adults with low basic skills and their higher skilled counterparts is lower than in other Nordic countries (Figure 4.10).

Figure 4.10. Employers in Finland frequently cover training cost of adults with low basic skills

Employed learners age 25-64 who reported that their employer paid course costs entirely, by skill level, %

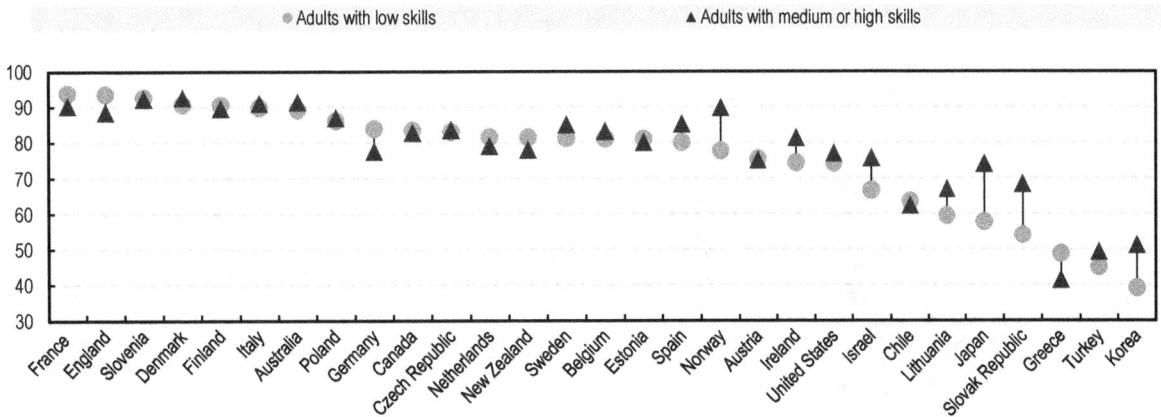

Note: Adults in dependent employment, excluding self-employed; formal or non-formal adult education; low-skilled defined as adults scoring at level 1 or below in literacy and/or numeracy in PIAAC; Belgium refers to Flanders, United Kingdom to England and Northern Ireland.
Source: PIAAC (2012, 2015).

Learning participation of unemployed adults with low skills

When unemployed, adults with low educational attainment participated less often in training-related ALMPs (self-motivated studies, vocational labour market training, work and education try out, job rotation and job search training) than higher qualified adults. They are far more likely to participate in rehabilitative work-experience, a measure typically aimed at the long-term unemployed to prevent disabilities and adapting work places to illness, injury or impairment (Figure 4.11).

An analysis of the labour market outcomes of participants shows that adults with low skills achieve the best results when participating in job rotation (fixed-term substitution of employees on job alternation leave). 59% of low-skilled adults are in employment three and six months after the end of programme participation, yet the overall share of low-skilled adults participating in the measure is low (1.2%). Relatively good labour market outcomes are also achieved by adults with low skills participating in vocational labour market training (31% are employed 3 or 6 months after participating). By contrast, self-motivated studies record the worst results (15% in employment following participation). Nearly twice as many adults with low skills participate in self-motivated studies than in labour market training. This highlights the relative importance of engaging adults with low skills in shorter labour-market relevant learning opportunities, although it should be noted that the existing data does not show a causal impact of participation on employment outcomes.

Figure 4.11. Adults with low basic skills do not participate in the ALMPs that yield the best outcomes for them

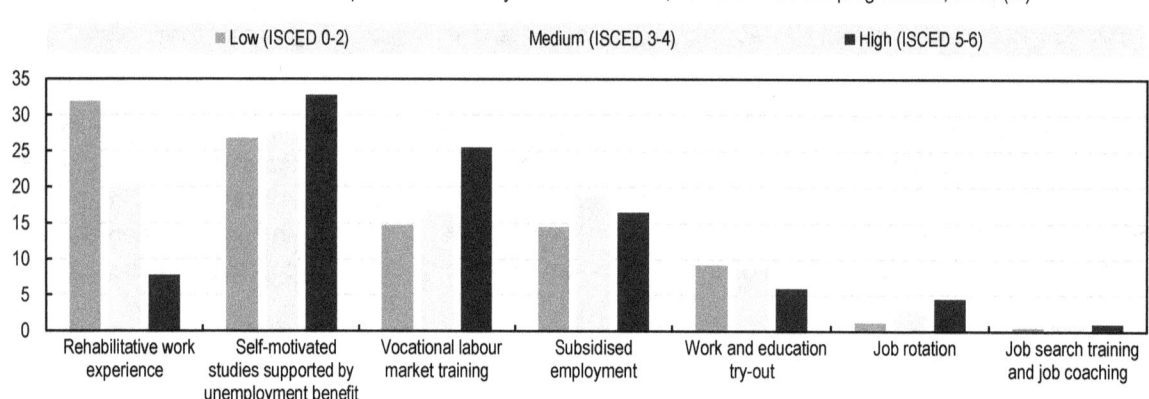

Panel A: Participation in ALMPs by level of education, distribution across programmes, 2018 (%)

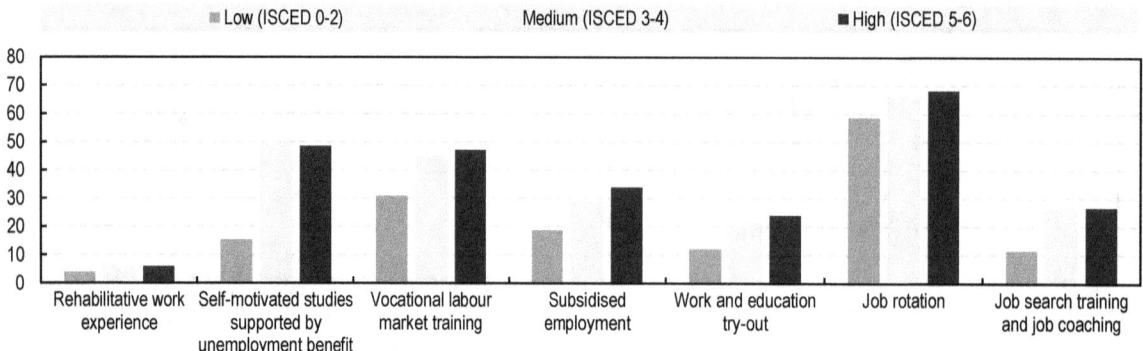

Panel B: Share of programme participants in employment three and six months after the end of the programme by programme and by level of education, 2016 (%)

Source: Ministry of Economic Affairs and Employment (2019), Tuomaala (2018[14]), "Aktiivisilta työvoimapoliittisilta palveluilta avoimille työmarkkinoille sijoittuminen".

Guidance and learning provision for adults with low basic skills

Given the universal and open nature of the Finnish adult learning system, adults with low skills have access to much of the adult learning provision outlined in Chapter 3. Adults with low skills have access to the same advice and guidance services as the general population. Partly as a result, there is very limited specific learning provision targeted at adults with low basic skills. However, low literacy proficiency and lack of learning skills constitute barriers to learning for this target group. Many may need to boost their basic skills first in order to take advantage of upskilling and reskilling opportunities for the general population. Finland is in the process of developing more comprehensive services for adults with low basic skills to cater to their specific needs.

Learning provision for adults with low basic skills

As discussed in Chapter 3, **formal education** in Finland is typically free or low-cost regardless of age. Several courses in formal education have the potential to attract and serve adults with low skills. Adults can complete comprehensive or upper secondary education and retake individual subjects to improve their grades. Taking VET degrees is open and free of charge for adults who completed primary and lower secondary education. However, entry to university level education is very competitive and typically out of reach for adults with low skills or low qualifications, although participation in Open University courses provides an entry route to university education for those without formal qualification.

Adults with low basic skills or educational attainment can also participate in **Adult Liberal Education**. Participation is voluntary; there are no entry requirements or prerequisites. Adult Education Centres provide recreational courses (such as cooking or photography) or lectures in certain topics (such as history or technology) based on learner interest. The offer increasingly includes courses to develop basic and job-related skills for specific target groups. For example, learning opportunities include basic digital skills for the elderly, such as on the use of smartphones, and the Adult Education Centre of Helsinki is experimenting with delivering basic skill training to a wider target group (i.e. reading, writing, basic numeracy and digital skills). In some cities, adult education centres were also assigned the role of providing language training for migrants. Participants in liberal adult education are often older, including retirees. As around half of the low skilled or low qualified are above the age of 55, liberal adult education may be an effective way to reach out to this group.

Job-related non-formal training of adults with low basic skills or low qualifications can also be initiated by employers or the public employment centre. As smaller companies are less likely to offer staff training opportunities (see Chapter 3), adults with low basic skills are in a disadvantaged position. On the other hand, joint purchase training (*Yhteishankintakoulutus*) can be a very relevant opportunity for this group. Tailored training can provide partially funded training to retrain employees. One target group of "change training" (*MuutosKoulutus*) is staff that is on the verge of redundancy, which overlaps to some extent with low-skilled jobs held by workers whose skills are obsolete. However, these streams currently provide training only to relatively few adults per year.

There is no countrywide programme in Finland that is targeted at improving the basic skills and learning motivation of adults with low basic skills. The NOSTE programme was one such programme, but it was discontinued in 2009 (Box 4.4).

> **Box 4.4. Basic skills training for adults**
>
> The **NOSTE** programme was implemented by the Ministry of Education and Culture between 2003 and 2009. It aimed to raise the educational attainment of adults without secondary education who were already in the labour market. The project was developed by the Finnish Parliamentary Adult Education and Training Committee based on prior analysis of the Finnish labour market and the situation of adults with low educational attainment. The goal was to improve the labour market prospects of this group by providing an opportunity to: attain a vocational upper secondary qualification or specialist vocational qualifications; undertake IT training; or finish initial education. An important project feature was to link education to the work environment.
>
> Participation was free of charge apart from examination fees. The total budget was EUR 124.5 million. The programme was delivered in the form of 59 regional projects provided by a network of various education institutions (vocational adult centres, folk high schools, upper secondary schools, job centres etc.). Outreach was identified as an important feature to increase the motivation of the target group. An overarching campaign was coordinated by the Central Organisation of Finnish Trade Unions (*SAK*) using around 10% of the total funds. In addition, teachers and programme coordinators also promoted the programme through, for example, company visits. Over the implementation period, the programme attracted 25 680 participants who gained almost 20 000 qualifications, reaching 73% of its initial target. The evaluation of the project found that it improved self-esteem and work motivation, but this failed to improve labour market outcomes (e.g. higher wages, new positions etc.). The programme increased awareness about the importance of adapting educational programmes to the low qualified and cooperation between stakeholders.
>
> The **Young Adults' Skills Programme** (NAO) was implemented between 2013-16 by the Ministry of Education and Culture. The target group of the programme was young adults aged 20-29 who did not have an upper secondary qualification, although between 2015 and 2016 the programme was also available to older adults. Education was provided at existing institutions using work-based methods and guidance and counselling. It also included outreach activities. The total budget was EUR 183 million to train around 4 000 people per year. The programme is considered successful in reaching the target number and reaching vulnerable groups.
>
> Source: Ministry of Education and Culture (2010[15]), "Noste Programme 2003-2009 Final Report", https://minedu.fi/en/publication?pubid=URN:ISBN:978-952-485-909-7; Antikainen (2014[16]), "NOSTE-programme for low-skilled adults", https://www.researchgate.net/publication/291818132; Ministry of Education and Culture (2017[17]), "Education guarantee and Young Adult's Skills Programme (NAO) in Finland 2013-2018"; Hyvönen (2016[18]), "Key findings and further development of the Young Adults' Skills programmes in Finland", https://epale.ec.europa.eu/fi/node/20740".

Advice and guidance services for adults with low basic skills

Advice and guidance on career and training choices for adults is primarily delivered by educational institutions, Public Employment Services and some specialised services that provide wrap-around support for specific target groups.

15 regional **Employment and Economic Development Offices (TE Offices)** deliver services to jobseekers (employed or unemployed) and employers in 120 branches across Finland. Registration with the PES is a precondition for receiving unemployment benefit or social assistance. Employment and business services are organised around three service lines for registered jobseekers: i) employment and entrepreneurship; ii) skill development; and iii) supported employment. Adults with low basic skills or qualifications are typically assigned to the second and third service lines as they are in need of education, training or rehabilitative work. When adults with low basic skills access services at the TE office, they first

get profiled based on an online tool and interviews, where their individual situation is assessed. There is no direct testing of skill levels. All individuals receive a personal development plan that has to be agreed between the jobseeker and the TE counsellor. There are periodical checks by the caseworker to follow up on the progress of the clients after three and six months of the initial interview. These can be undertaken in-person, by phone or video link (Finn, 2016[19]). However, the caseload of TE counsellors is very high, typically leaving very limited time per client and not always the time to regularly check-in on them.

The Finnish public employment service also provides services for some disadvantaged groups in the form of **Multi-Sectoral Joint Services (TYP) Centers**. Across Finland 34 such centres provide complex services under one roof with the cooperation of the Municipalities, the Public Employment Service (TE) and the Social Insurance Institution (KELA). These include health care, social and rehabilitative services together with support entering the labour market. The target group is the long-term unemployed with some exceptions (e.g. young adults below 25, who are unemployed for more than 6 months). As almost half of low-skilled and low-educated adults are inactive, these centres have the potential to cover a significant share of the group. There is no active outreach activity carried out by the centres themselves. Instead, the TE refers clients to the TYP centres, where following an intensive mapping phase of maximum 3 months, each of the clients receive a personalised multi-sectoral employment plan agreed between the jobseeker, the TE and the municipal social worker (if assigned to the case). This plan clarifies the tasks and responsibilities of the different agencies. According to the MoEE between 2016 and 2018 an average of 19 000 adults were enrolled in multi sectoral joint services per year (Finn, 2016[19]).

Municipalities have also introduced specific multi-service centres for migrants, such as the **Helsinki Skills Center** (*Stadin osaamiskeskus*). Similar centres exist in other bigger cities such as Vantaa, Espoo, Turku and Tampere. Here, public employment services (TE office) work together with the municipality to streamline provision that results in more effective integration. The goal is to find well-matched jobs for the clients or, if not possible, help them enrol in education. Activities start with mapping the skills and qualifications of the clients through interviews and then drawing up personalised integration and learning plans. The clients can be referred to language training, basic skill training, vocational education or job coaching. Support is available in multiple languages such as Arabic, Somali or English. All immigrants over 17, who are registered with the TE office as jobseekers living in the Helsinki area can access the services. Clients are typically referred from the TE offices with few exceptions (one ESF-funded programme run by the centre targets stay at home parents). The centre started operating in 2016 and serves around 1 000 clients annually. (City of Helsinki, 2018[20]; Winsten, 2019[21]).

Ongoing experimentation to improve service provision

In order to conduct the basic income experiment, the Finnish government adopted a law in 2017 that allows for experimentation in developing better public services. Increasing the culture of public sector innovation overall was an explicit goal of the outgoing government. Experimental Finland (*Kokeileva Suomi*) was established in 2016 as part of the Prime Minister's Office to spread this approach. Since then many experiments have been put in place, including in the area of adult education with special attention on those with low basic skills (Prime Minister's Office, 2019[22]).

The ESF-funded **Taito** programme aims to improve basic skills (literacy, numeracy, digital skills) of those with low levels of skills, and thus help them advance in education and training and in working life (OECD, 2019[23]). This programme is composed of multiple small-scale projects selected by the Ministry of Education and Culture for the purpose of experimentation and to understand which ones are the most effective (EAEA, 2017[24]). These projects aim to improve skills of students, as well as different groups of adults, e.g. migrants, inactive, low qualified. These are implemented by different stakeholders such as universities, research organisations, associations or education centres. Some examples targeted at adults include developing an effective tutor model, creating a toolkit for improving basic skills at the workplace or developing a model to map basic skills. As part of the project, the **TAIKOJA** network coordinates between projects, collects good practices and finds ways to incorporate these into the educational structure. This network is managed jointly between the Häme University of Applied Sciences, Omnia, the OK Study Centre and the University of Tampere (TAIKOJA, 2019[25]).

The Ministry of Economic Affairs and Employment has been implementing a number of experiments to test different tools or service delivery methods. **Regional Employment Trials** were implemented at eight different locations, covering around 45 000 jobseekers, to improve PES services and increase employment levels. The reason for implementing the trials was partly to prepare for the planned regional government reform (which did not pass); therefore, municipalities typically had a central role. Good practices included increased collaboration between stakeholders at the local level, more personalised support for job seekers, more intensive case-management or the use of new digital devices. These practices were then reused when designing the new **TE Service Pilots**. These new pilots can be grouped in two main categories. One is to provide better services for businesses, including recruitment and training practices (e.g. establishing a Knowledge Profiling Platform that identifies ICT skill needs). The second is to improve services for people in vulnerable positions (e.g. the disabled). The pilots are based on cooperation between ELY Centres, TE Offices, KELA, education providers, associations and companies to ensure smooth service provision. The outcomes will be evaluated in 2020/2021 (Tiina Korhonen, 2018[26]; Ministry of Economic Affairs and Employment, 2019[27]).

Key challenges

The comparatively large inequality in participation in Finland between adults with low basic skills and those with higher skills suggests that there are some structural issues holding back participation of adults with low skills. Barriers to accessing learning provision are already low in Finland, with much of the provision being offered for free or at a low-cost to the individual and delivered flexibly. After careful analysis of the Finnish system and the characteristics and needs of adults with low basic skills the following key challenges emerge: i) gaps in the provision of comprehensive advice and guidance services; ii) lack of targeted education provision; and iii) limited outreach activities.

Adults with low basic skills need more comprehensive advice and guidance services.

Low skilled adults face more complex obstacles to participation than their higher skilled counterparts do. Data shows that the primary obstacle to training participation for adults with low basic skills is lack of time due to work (18%) and family (12%) responsibilities (Figure 4.12.). Compared with medium or higher skilled adults in Finland, those with low skills face less work-related and more family-related obstacles. This may be linked to the fact that a higher share of them are not in employment. It can also be more difficult for them to outsource domestic responsibilities (e.g. cooking or childcare) due to a relatively low income. As demonstrated earlier, many low-skilled adults are also low wage earners. It is not surprising that the lack of financial resources constitute a key obstacle for 9% of adults with low-skills, much higher than for those with medium/high skills (2%). They tend to have less savings and can expect limited support from their families.

Compared with other Nordic (and even more so OECD) countries, low-skilled Finns are more likely to list lack of employer support or prerequisites as barriers to participation, which may point to issues regarding flexibility of continuous learning in working life. Individuals with low basic skills often have lower bargaining power vis-à-vis their employers. Their work is more easily substitutable and employers are afraid of their workers being poached once they invest in their skill development. The Finnish working-life barometer confirms this lower training investment by employers; there is a 30 percentage point participation gap between white-collar and lower-skilled manual workers.

Figure 4.12. Barriers to participation differ between low and higher skilled adults

Reasons for not participating in learning for those who wanted to participate, Finland and Nordic countries, %

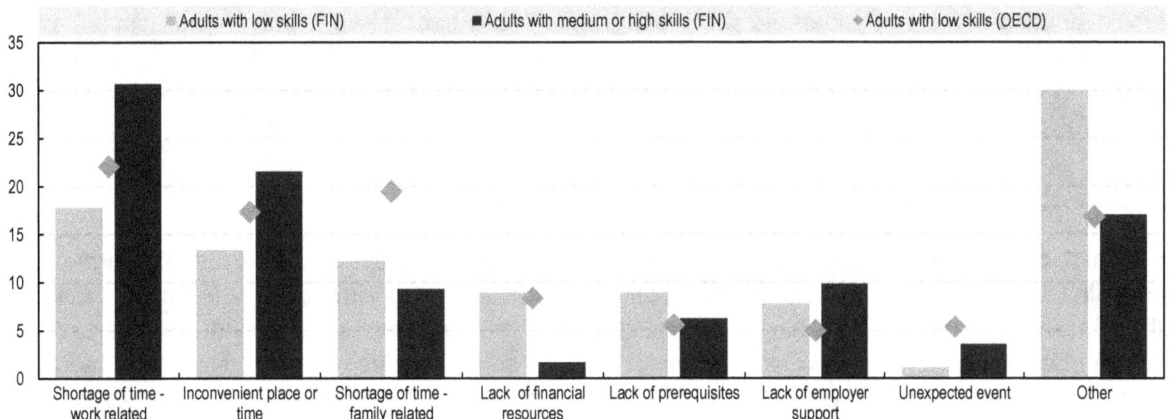

Note: Formal or non-formal adult education in the past 12 months; low-skilled defined as adults scoring at level 1 or below in literacy and/or numeracy in PIAAC; Nordic countries refer to Denmark, Norway and Sweden without Finland.
Source: PIAAC (2012).

Around one third of adults with low basic skills claimed that they did not participate due to 'other reasons', which points to the diverse set of obstacles they face. Such additional reasons can be fatigue, not finding appropriate opportunities, health problems or fear of failure. According to the Adult Education Survey, 24% of adults with low qualifications in Finland reported health or age as a reason for not participating in adult education. This is in line with other findings that adults in Nordic countries face fewer situational (e.g. lack of time) and institutional (e.g. lack of prerequisites or high fees) barriers than in other countries (Roosmaa and Saar, 2017[28]).

The above-mentioned barriers exist on top of any barriers related to navigating the education and training system. Information is fragmented and understanding the rules around financial support can be challenging for many. Lower literacy proficiency makes it more difficult to process and analyse the vast amount of information available and to make good training decisions (OECD, 2019[3]). Those, who do not participate in education often have little or low knowledge about available opportunities. Many for example believe that education is always formal, inflexible, exam-oriented and classroom-based. This highlights the need for guidance services for this group. Another characteristic of adults with low basic skills in general is that they tend to face multiple barriers at the same time (as opposed to higher skilled people, who can typically pinpoint one) and what is deterring them is the cumulative effect of these (Pennacchia et al., 2018[29]). Comprehensive advice and guidance services that address the complex barriers of adults with low-skills are therefore critical to engage them in training. However, there are currently a number of gaps in the provision of these services in Finland.

Career guidance opportunities for low skilled adults in working life are limited. Adults with low basic skills might not be able to benefit fully from written and online resources (due to the lack of literacy or digital skills), and may need more in-person support. However, adults typically only get in touch with guidance services in TE offices once job-loss has already happened. Meanwhile career guidance services for the employed that could help to navigate the educational opportunities are limited, raising efficiency concerns. The current high client per caseworker ratio at TE-offices is especially problematic for disadvantaged groups, such as adults with low basic skills who need more encouragement, information and face-time (Windisch, 2016[30]). Guidance can also be offered at the workplace, but adults with low basic skills, who are typically in jobs with little development opportunities, are not likely to have access to such support.

Services that intend to provide comprehensive solutions for the complex barriers of this group are not available for all adults with low skills. One-stop shops were introduced to provide integrated and tailored information and guidance for youngsters and migrants (*Ohjaamo, Stadin osaamiskeskus*), however these target groups constitute less than 20% of low-skilled adults in Finland. Multi-service centres for long-term unemployed also cover a considerable share of adults with low basic skills, although individuals have to spend 12-month in unemployment before having access to such services. Counselling at TE offices tend to focus only on labour-market related issues instead of having the systematic overview that multi-service centres provide. An important challenge remains how to establish multi-service centres in smaller cities.

Targeted education provision for adults with low skills is lacking.

The Finnish continuous learning system is designed to be universal, open and permeable. In principle, adults with low basic skills or qualifications can take part in many of the formal and non-formal courses as well as in employer-provided training. However, adults with low basic skills do not always have the necessary basic skills to undertake such training. Specific competencies such as literacy are needed to generate new ones through learning (Desjardins, Rubenson and Milana, 2006[31]). For example to retrain as a nurse, they would probably need higher literacy and numeracy skills than Level 2.

Therefore, the strong and increasing focus on formal education may deter adults with low basic skills from participating. Having to participate in lengthy – often classroom-based studies – can be perceived as a large time and resource investment that sets a high threshold for participation. In fact, data shows that adults with low basic skills are more than three times less likely than those with high skill levels to participate in formal education (5% vs. 16% respectively). This is larger than the participation gap for non-formal education (29% vs. 66% respectively) (Figure 4.13.). Interestingly, even when educational leave and financial support are both available (such as during self-motivated studies supported by the adult education allowance), the take-up of formal education by adults with low skill levels is low (Kauhanen, 2018[32]). This signals that there are some specific features of formal studies that deter adults with low basic skills from participating, which is especially problematic in Finland where participation in formal education is highly valued.

Figure 4.13. Very few Finnish adults with low basic skills take part in formal education.

Adults age 25-65 who participated in different types of learning by skill level, Finland, %

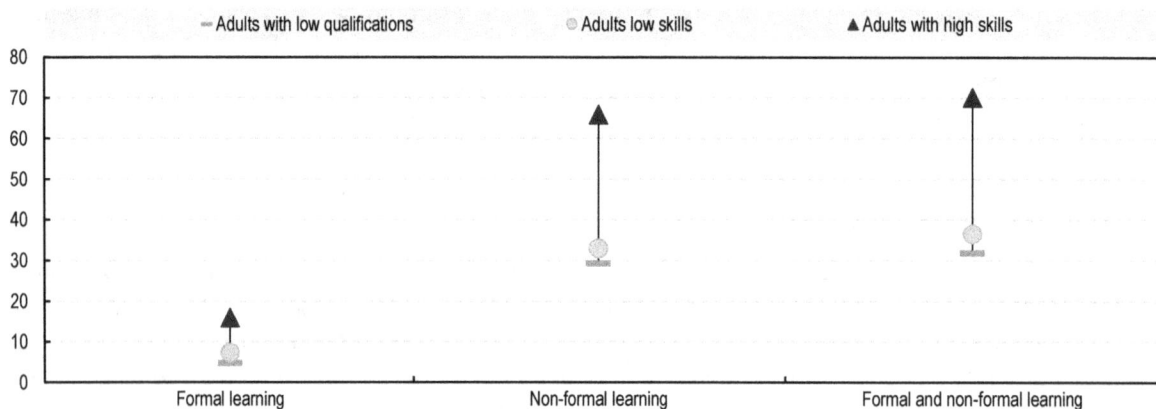

Note: Low-skilled defined as adults scoring at level 1 or below in literacy and/or numeracy in PIAAC. Low qualified refers to those, whose highest educational attainment is ISCED Level 0-2. Formal and non-formal learning participation is the sum of both learning activities (adults who participated in both are counted only once).
Source: PIAAC (2012).

The flipside of the universal and open nature of Finnish adult learning provision is that it rarely targets specific population groups directly. In contrast to many other OECD economies, there is currently no countrywide programme that aims to increase learning motivation of adults with low basic skills and to systematically support them in the acquisition of basic skills. Yet, the evidence suggests that adults, in particular those with low basic skills, need education opportunities that are tailored to their specific learning needs, because they learn differently than children and young people. They learn best when learning is practical, problem-oriented and contextualised, i.e. linked to experiences in an adults' work or personal life such as calculating prices at the supermarket (Windisch, 2016[30]; OECD, 2019[3]). Following from this, the lack of shorter, job-related and recognised adult learning provision in Finland is likely to deter many adults with low basic skills from engaging in continuous learning activities.

Outreach activities to engage adults with low-skills in learning are limited.

Even if appropriate education opportunities are available, adults with low basic skills might not take them up. One of the key reasons behind this is lack of awareness of their learning needs. Research suggests that adults compare their skill levels with a 'local standard', i.e. those of their colleagues, friends and family surrounding them, making it more difficult to recognise where their skills fall short (Finnie and Meng, 2005[33]). Moreover, as weak basic skills such as literacy problems often have a stigma attached to them, adults can be reluctant to reveal their lack of skills or express interest in learning opportunities in this area (Windisch, 2016[30]). Indeed, adults with low qualifications are generally far less likely to search for information on learning opportunities than those with medium or higher qualifications. While the share of adults with low qualifications looking for information is highest in Finland out of EU countries, they still do so far less than adults with higher qualifications (Figure 4.14). This highlights the need for targeted outreach activities for adults with low basic skills.

Figure 4.14. Adults with low skills are less likely to seek out information on learning opportunities

Adults age 25-64 who searched for information on learning opportunities, by educational attainment level, 2016, %

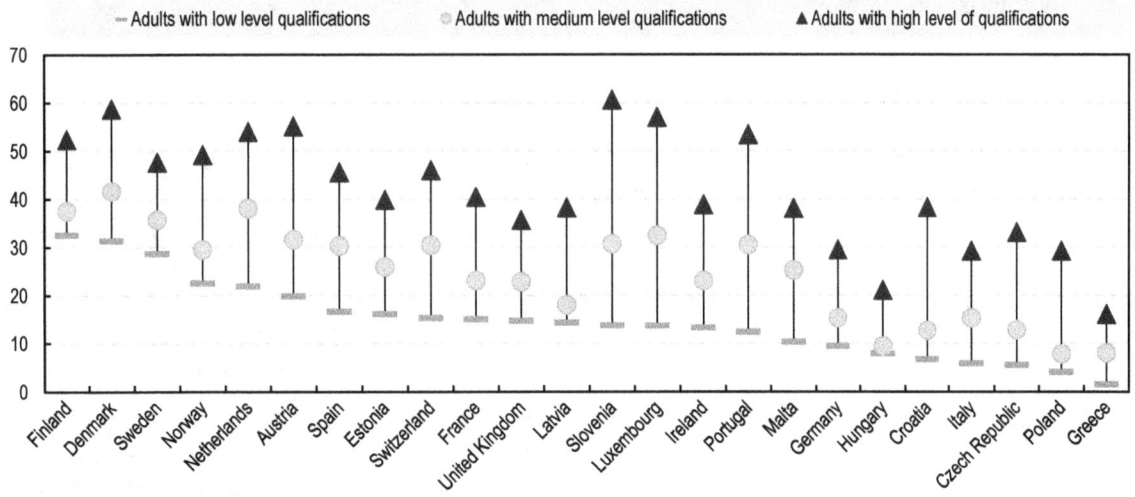

Note: Search for information on learning possibilities by type of learning and educational attainment level. Low qualifications refer to ISCED 0-2, medium to ISCED 3-4 and high to ISCED 5-8.
Source: Eurostat, Adult Education Survey (2016).

As the Finnish adult learning provision is universal and open to adults with all skill levels in principle, it is often seen as being the choice of individuals to seek out and participate in learning activities. Therefore, outreach activities are not structurally embedded across the Finnish labour market. Guidance and education institutions do not get specific funding to conduct outreach and rely on referrals from other institutions, e.g. the PES. Exceptions exist, for example the *Helsinki Skills Centre*, which reaches out to stay-at home parents with migrant background in community spaces, such as butcher shops. Similarly, the *Ohjamoo* centres intend to set-up mobile counselling services in shopping malls in the future. The evaluation of the programme underlined the importance of the personal contact for its success (Ministry of Education and Culture, 2010[15]).

Policy recommendations and good practices

The Finnish adult education system must recognise and cater to the specific needs of adults with low basic skills to increase their participation in learning. To overcome the key challenges, Finland should consider: i) providing comprehensive information and guidance services; ii) developing tailored education programmes; and iii) reaching out to adults with low basic skills.

Some of the recommendations would require additional funds. Reallocation of some of the general funding for adult learning to activities for adults with low basic skills would improve efficiency. Introducing additional funding streams such as training levies could also be considered.

Provide comprehensive information and guidance services

Recommendations

Currently, information and guidance that helps adults with low basic skills to overcome the multiple barriers they face to learning is not comprehensively available. To ensure that all adults with low basic skills can up-skill continuously, Finland could benefit from:

1. Further developing one-shop-shops that provide comprehensive advice and guidance;
2. Strengthening the capacity of TE offices.

Further develop one-stop-shops that provide comprehensive advice and guidance

Adults with low basic skills need assistance in addressing their often cumulative barriers to training participation, such as funding, childcare or health issues. Information and guidance is most effective when all information can be accessed under one roof and is tailored to individual circumstances. Finland should consider expanding such services for all adults with low basic skills, building on the positive outcomes of one-stop-shops and multi-service delivery for migrants, youth and long-term unemployed individuals. Rather than introducing specific one-stop-shops for adults with low-skills, consider whether these services can be streamlined to prevent further fragmentation of the advice and guidance system.

Any future development must be informed by the experience of existing one-stop shops in Finland (e.g. *Ohjaamo, Helsinki Skills Centre, Multi-service delivery to long-term unemployed*) as well as the outcomes of ongoing experiments *(TE Service Pilots)*. Challenges include: the coordination of different information systems in multi-service delivery; aligning approaches and working-culture of individuals from different service-delivery backgrounds; outreach to involve underserved groups of the population; and the need for the involvement of health services to serve disadvantaged target groups.

Important lessons can also be drawn from other OECD countries looking to streamline advice and guidance services and to provide one-stop-shop solutions for this target group:

- **Provide high quality guidance:** In Iceland demand for career development for employed adults has been growing in recent years. Public Employment Service offices provide free career guidance to all adults, while advice at regional *Lifelong Learning Centres* is also available for all, although only fully funded for the low qualified. There are a dozen of *Lifelong Learning Centres* around Iceland including in sparsely populated areas. The strength of these centres is considered to be their highly qualified staff who typically hold degrees in education and vocational counselling and as a result are able to tailor the services to each client. Apart from knowledge about labour market needs and education opportunities, counsellors are trained to provide comprehensive guidance on financial and health issues amongst others. The centres are accredited through the European Quality Mark (EQM) system, which was developed through an EU funded projects in cooperation with countries and local stakeholders. The centres apply for funding annually regarding their specific measures (e.g. career guidance, development of job standards or educational pathways). The annual cost of career guidance provided at the centres for low-qualified adults was approximately ISK 134 million (equivalent to EUR 1 Mio.) for around 10 000 sessions in 2016 (Ministry of Education Science and Culture Iceland, 2018[34]; OECD, 2019[3]).
- **Expand free counselling services**: In Austria career information services are available to all adults seeking advice. The *Bildungsberatung Österreich* offers independent and free counselling for adults on education and training opportunities. The service is implemented in all Austrian federal states and specifically targets adults with disadvantages in the labour market, including the low-skilled, older adults, inactive and adults with a migrant background. Depending on the federal state, advice and guidance services are provided in a range of modes, including face-to-face, on the phone or online via skype or chat. To open the service to individuals with migrant background the service is provided in 16 languages, although not all languages are spoken in every location. Since 2012, more than 100 guidance practitioners have been trained and qualified to provide advice. The project is financed by the ESF and the Austrian Ministry of Education.

A key question in the Finnish context is how to bring such complex services to smaller cities and sparsely populated areas in a cost-effective way:

- **Provide mobile services**: The Brussels-based project Formtruck is a walk-in mobile information centre on training opportunities. It aims to engage low-qualified jobseekers and young people not in employment, education or training. Since its introduction in 2017, it has been used around 20 times per year, although there are no evaluations on the effectiveness of this approach. Mobile outreach services have the possibility to reach those adults with low skills such as long-term unemployed who have very limited links to workplaces or the community. It can also be helpful in delivering services in rural areas in a cost-effective way.

Strengthen the capacity of the TE-offices

Currently, public employment services are one of the key entry points for adults with low skills who seek employment and career advice. However, TE-offices are struggling with the high caseload of their counsellors and lack capacity to provide comprehensive advice and guidance service for this target group. In the early 2010s, TE-offices were reorganised involving significant staff cuts. Since then much of the interaction with TE-clients has shifted to email or phone contact. While the move towards digital and distance services is progressive in principle, it may not be the most appropriate form of interaction with this target group. It makes it more difficult to assess the real situation of this specific target group, e.g. in the case of health or behavioural issues that are not easily detected without face-to-face contact.

Finland should strengthen the role of public employment services and recognise their importance as a first port-of call for significant shares of adults with low-skills. This will require significant financial investments and reversing some of the financial cuts the PES has experienced over the past decade.

Develop tailored education programmes

> **Recommendations**
>
> Finland should consider the introduction of a targeted programme to improve the learning motivation and the skill levels of adults with low basic skills. To be successful, the programme must be easy to access, low cost or free of charge, not too time intensive and provided flexibly outside working hours. Some stakeholders suggest that the Liberal Adult Education system may be well placed to deliver such programmes, making use of their well-known brand, nation-wide coverage and strong links with the local community. Other options include the provision of contextualised learning of basic skills, for example in the workplace. To ensure that education opportunities are relevant and useful for adults with low skills, Finland could benefit from:
>
> 1. Developing a programme of short courses that aim to improve motivation towards learning;
> 2. Contextualising the learning activity.

Develop a programme of short courses that aim to improve motivation towards learning

Shorter courses that are adapted to adults with low skills are currently lacking from the menu of Finnish continuous learning provision. Even the discontinued NOSTE programme that was developed specifically for adults with low qualifications provided longer, typically formal educational opportunities with 6 months of average duration, while evidence underlines that adults with low-skills are less willing to participate in time-intensive training than high-skilled individuals (Fouarge, Schils and de Grip, 2013[35]).

Short 'taster' courses can provide an entryway for adults with low skills to rekindle their interest in education. To counter potential negative education experiences of the target group, courses should move away from some features of the initial education system and adapt provision to adults. As developing an adult learner's sense of confidence and competence is crucial, programmes should improve motivation and curiosity without putting too much emphasis on measuring learning outcomes with grading or exams, which entail the possibility of failure (O'Neill and Thomson, 2013[36]). Adults with low skills tend to learn better when the learning content is hands-on and problem-oriented and show greater motivation for topics that they see to be relevant and useful in daily activities (e.g. health, parenting or everyday finances).

Some OECD countries have introduced specific education offers for adults with low skills:

- **Establish a positive attitude to learning:** In Hungary, a network of Open Learning Centres provide low threshold training opportunities for adults with low basic skills or competencies. Centres are at accessible locations and designed to have a relaxed atmosphere. They are equipped with modern digital devices such as digital boards, smartphones and laptops, that can be used by people who walk-in. The learning centres offer educational opportunities in different topics, all of them are 20-30 hours long. Topics include household economics, green energy in everyday life, effective self-management or the role of women in the 21st century. The curriculum and learning materials were developed by experts, and designed specifically for adults with low basic skills. The teaching methods put emphasis on respecting and involving the participants through discussions and group exercises, which help to develop social and communication skills. Cooperation is favoured over competition; participants are encouraged to help each other outside of the courses and there are no grades or examination at the end. Centres can also create additional learning opportunities depending on the needs and interests of the community in the form of courses or even discussions and lectures. The overall goal is to increase motivation towards education and create a culture of curiosity and self-development. Since the programme in 2012, more than 10 000 people participated in the learning activities of the centres. As the model was designed to operate

- **Ensure quality of basic skill programmes**: The Austrian *Initiative Adult Education* was introduced in 2012 to enable individuals to obtain basic competences (literacy, numeracy) and educational qualifications (typically primary or lower secondary) free of charge. Only those education providers can apply for funding whom the Austrian Federal Ministry of Education accredits. The observed quality aspects are; adaption of courses to the needs of adults, course quality and qualification of trainers and counsellors. The approval also depends on the needs of the region to create a balance between the various courses. In addition to education, the initiative also provides support services such as professional counselling (looking holistically at the life situation of the individuals), an introduction phase and the individualisation of the learning offer. The programme is based on a cooperation between the federation (*Bund*) and the federal states (*Bundeslaender*). It is funded by a mix of national and ESF funds. Between 2012-2017 approximately 50 000 individuals participated in the measure. The initiative is now in its third programming period (Jenewein, 2018[38]; Steiner et al., 2017[39]; Steuerungsgruppe Initiative Erwachsenenbildung, 2019[40])

in a cost-effective way with low operational costs, some of the centres are in small villages (OECD, forthcoming[37]).

Contextualise the learning activity

In the delivery of a potential 'taster' learning programme for adults with low basic skills, Finland should consider linking the programme to everyday aspects of adults' lives, such as the workplace, or a community.

- **Combine basic skill training with job-related content:** With the majority of low-skilled adults in employment, one key option is to embed delivery in the workplace. A good practice in this area is the *Norwegian Skills Plus Work* programme, which provides grants for enterprises that train their employees by combining job-related with basic skill training with basic skills training while at the same time strengthening the worker's motivation to learn. The programme concentrates on reading, writing, numeracy and digital skills, and more recently oral communication. Firms work with providers to create basic skill programmes in these domains tailored to the needs of both the employers and the employees. Overall guidance is available on how to set up such programmes in the form of learning materials and national standards. The programme is open to both private and public companies and there is special effort to encourage SMEs and applications from industries that tend to have a higher share of low-skilled workers. The programme is funded by the Ministry of Education and Research and is administered by the Norwegian Agency for Lifelong Learning (*Kompetanse Norge*). It is considered an expensive but successful programme in reaching individuals who otherwise would not participate in learning activities (OECD, 2019[3]).
- **Making use of the family context:** There is also growing evidence of the positive effects of family literacy programmes on adult participants' self-efficacy and social capital, although more research on the long-term impact is needed to prove long-lasting benefits (Windisch, 2016[30]). The Austrian *Mum is learning German!* (Mama lernt Deutsch!) takes place in the child's educational institution and includes free childcare services, while parents learn or go on excursions to cultural, social and leisure institutions together. Data is not available on student performance, but there is positive outcome in terms of school climate and school-parent communication and the programme is widely accepted among headmasters, teachers and parents (OECD, 2018[6]).

Reach out to adults with low basic skills

> ## Recommendations
>
> Even where appropriate learning opportunities exist, adults with low skills might not take them up. They need more encouragement and awareness raising through outreach activities, however such activities are not structurally embedded in the Finnish system. To ensure that more adults with low skills find and participate in the appropriate training opportunities, Finland could benefit from:
>
> 1. Reaching out to adults with low skills;
> 2. Improving the understanding of the target group by collecting and analysing data.

Reach out to adults with low skills

Research evidence suggests that active and direct outreach is essential to successfully engage adults with low skills in learning, as public awareness campaigns have proven ineffective for this target group (OECD, 2019[3]). Outreach involves the provision of mobile services, awareness raising and referral to existing stationary services. It meets the underserved population of adults with low basic skills in their regular environment, such as their workplace or community.

To date, adult learning provision in Finland has devoted limited attention and resources to outreach, apart from the NOSTE programme. Some isolated good examples also exist such as the KYKY programme of the Helsinki Skills Centre. Finland should draw on domestic experience that proved to be effective:

- **Provide information and encouragement in person**: The NOSTE programme dedicated 10% of the funds on outreach activities. Awareness raising took place in radio advertisements, through online articles and a printed Nosetta magazine. The programme also had a truck that did road shows around Finland, promoting the programme. Apart from the centralised outreach activities, teachers and coordinators also allocated some of their time to outreach for example in the form of company visits. These discussions allowed them to clarify available adult learning opportunities, ensuring sensitivity to the needs of the individuals as well as assessing their current competence level. According to follow-up research, common features of effective outreach activities include direct, personal contacts, a multi-channel approach and peer activities. The programme evaluation also confirmed that the target group needed more encouragement and support than the average (especially at the beginning of the studies). (Ministry of Education and Culture, 2010[15]; Antikainen, 2014[16])

- **Find creative ways to engage a community**: One of the target groups of the *Helsinki Skills Centre's* programme KYKY (*Koulujen Yritysten Kiihdytetty Yhteiskehittäminen*) are stay-at-home parents who typically do not get in touch with authorities. Main target groups are Somali, Kurdish and Arabic speaking migrants. Outreach takes place with the help of municipalities, NGOs, language-learning groups, but also by approaching individuals about the programme in food shops that are frequented by immigrants. The programme employs counsellors from the community, as it was recognised that personal contact and word of mouth was key to engaging participants. One of the key learnings from the programme is that the target population needs to be sufficiently large for community engagement to be effective (min. 3000 people). The programme is funded by the European Social Fund and it is operational since 2014. (Winsten, 2019[21])

There are many ways to connect with adults in their day-to-day lives with the goal to inform and signpost them to learning opportunities. Outreach is especially successful when it makes use of existing relationships of those who know the target group, such as trade unions, teachers NGOs or social workers

(Human Resources and Social Development Canada, 2008[41]). Existing practices from other OECD economies illustrate how this can work in practice:

- **Reach out in the workplace:** The trade union-led programme *Unionlearn* in the UK trains Union Learning Representatives who promote the value of learning in companies, support learners in identifying their training needs and arrange education and basic skill training opportunities. The programme also intends to build learner confidence through peer-to-peer support. It makes use of the existing relationship and trust between workers and their trade union representatives. Since its inception in the 1990s, Unionlearn has helped adults to achieve self-confidence, career progression and further training participation. Employers also recognise benefits such as an increase in organisational performance. Evaluation results show that the programme is especially successful for those with low skills, older workers and learners from minority ethnic groups. The programme is funded by the Union Learning Fund, which receives GBP 12 million from the Department for Education per year. It has been estimated that every pound invested in the programme has brought a return of GBP 12.3 to the economy (OECD, 2019[3]; Pennacchia et al., 2018[29]).

- **Engage adults where their children are learning:** The Austrian *Mum is learning German!* (Mama lernt Deutsch!) programme is also a good example in this regard. The programme provides basic skills courses for mothers with low-educational levels and for whom German is not their first language. Courses take place at their children's basic education institution and reaches out to adults in their role as parents. The programme recognises that many adults are confronted with their own low literacy and numeracy levels when their child enters education, which provides them with a reason to take up learning (OECD, 2019[3]).

Improve understanding of the target group by collecting and analysing data

Effective outreach relies on a good understanding of the target group, ideally based on quantitative and qualitative data. Currently, Finland is lacking comprehensive data on participation of adults with low basic skills in different kinds of education provision. It will be important to improve the knowledge base on the characteristics and participation patterns of adults with low basic skills to improve outreach activities in the future. A forthcoming OECD report on monitoring participation in adult learning programmes provides some good examples in the field (OECD, forthcoming[42]):

- **Establish a database along with targeted programmes:** Linked to the Norwegian Skills Plus programme, a database has been created to improve monitoring. The database includes detailed information on participants (gender, formal education, industry etc.), which helps to ensure that the programme reaches the intended target groups. The database is also expected to provide a basis for evaluating the outcomes and the long-term impact of the programme.

- **Enable a linking of participant's data to other databases**: In Sweden, municipalities offer adult education courses at the basic and upper secondary level (*Komvux*). A database (*Komvuxdatabasen*) contains statistics on participation in these courses including course completion, grades, continuing education and personal characteristics (e.g. age, education, gender, country of birth). Information is available by year, subject, level and municipality. This database can be complemented with the Longitudinal Integrated Database for Health Insurance and Labour Market Studies (*LISA*) to obtain information on even more individual characteristics, transfer payments and earnings. Individuals are identified thanks to their personal identity number (*personnummer*). The municipalities submit the data to Statistics Sweden, which handles the management of the data on behalf of the Swedish National Agency for Education for Formal Education.

References

Antikainen, A. (2014), *NOSTE-programme for low-skilled adults*, https://www.researchgate.net/publication/291818132. [16]

City of Helsinki (2018), *Helsinki Skill Centre*, https://www.hel.fi/maahanmuuttajat/en/work-and-entrerpise/helsinki-skill-center/. [20]

Desjardins, R., K. Rubenson and M. Milana (2006), *Unequal chances to participate in adult learning: international perspectives*, UNESCO. [31]

EAEA (2017), *Adult education in Europe 2017, a civicl society view*. [24]

Finn, D. (2016), *Issues emerging from combining active and passive measures for the long term unemployed - the design and delivery of single points of contact*, European Commission. [19]

Finnie, R. and R. Meng (2005), "Literacy and labour market outcomes: Self-assessment versus test score measures", *Applied Economics*, Vol. 37/17, pp. 1935-1951, http://dx.doi.org/10.1080/00036840500244519. [33]

Flisi, S. et al. (2018), "Cohort patterns in adult literacy skills: How are new generations doing?", *Journal of Policy Modeling*, http://dx.doi.org/10.1016/j.jpolmod.2018.10.002. [5]

Fouarge, D., T. Schils and A. de Grip (2013), "Why do low-educated workers invest less in further training?", *Applied Economics*, Vol. 45/18, pp. 2587-2601, http://dx.doi.org/10.1080/00036846.2012.671926. [35]

Goto, S. and C. Martin (2009), "Psychology of Success: Overcoming Barriers to Pursuing Further Education", *The Journal of Continuing Higher Education*, Vol. 57/1, pp. 10-21, http://dx.doi.org/10.1080/07377360902810744. [13]

Hillage, J. and J. Aston (2001), *Attracting new learners - a literature review*, Learning and Skill Development Agency, London, https://eric.ed.gov/?id=ED466991. [9]

Human Resources and Social Development Canada (2008), *A Look At Best Practices for Conducting Outreach for Literacy Programs*. [41]

Hyvönen, E. (2016), *Key findings and further development of the Young Adults' Skills programmes in Finland*, EPALE Website, https://epale.ec.europa.eu/fi/node/20740 (accessed on 16 December 2019). [18]

Jenewein, F. (2018), "Sechs Jahre Basisbildung im Rahmen der Initiative Erwachsenenbildung", *Magazin Erwachsenenbildung*, Vol. 33, http://www.erwachsenenbildung.at/magazin (accessed on 12 July 2019). [38]

Kauhanen, A. (2018), "The Effects of an Education-Leave Program on Educational Attainment and Labor-Market Outcomes", *ETLA Working Papers*, http://pub.etla.fi/ETLA-Working-Papers-56.pdf. [32]

Lavecchia, A., H. Liu and P. Oreopoulos (2015), *Behavioral Economics of Education: Progress and Possibilities*. [10]

Ministry of Economic Affairs and Employment (2019), *Kasvupalvelupiloteista TE-palvelupilotteihin*. [27]

Ministry of Education and Culture (2017), *Education guarantee and Young Adult´s Skills Programme (NAO) in Finland 2013-2018*. [17]

Ministry of Education and Culture (2010), *Noste Programme 2003-2009 Finlan Report*, http://www.minedu.fi /OPM/Julkaisut/julkaisulistaus?lang=en. [15]

Ministry of Education Science and Culture Iceland (2018), *Policy Questionnaire: Readiness of Adult Learning Systems to Address Changing Skills Needs*. [34]

Musset, P. (2015), *Building Skills For All: A Review of Finland. Policy Insights on literacy, numeracy and digital skills from the survey of adult skills*, OECD, Paris, http://www.oecd.org/finland/Building-Skills-For-All-A-Review-of-Finland.pdf (accessed on 19 April 2019). [2]

Norden (2015), *Adult Skills in the Nordic Region*, Nordic Council of Ministers, http://www.norden.org. [8]

OECD (2019), *Getting Skills Right: Engaging low-skilled adults in learning*, OECD, Paris, http://www.oecd.org/employment/emp/engaging-low-skilled-adults-2019.pdf. [3]

OECD (2019), *Getting Skills Right: Future-Ready Adult Learning Systems*, Getting Skills Right, OECD Publishing, Paris, https://dx.doi.org/10.1787/9789264311756-en. [23]

OECD (2018), *Working Together: Skills and Labour Market Integration of Immigrants and their Children in Finland*, OECD Publishing, Paris, https://dx.doi.org/10.1787/9789264305250-en. [6]

OECD (forthcoming), *Increasing Adult Learning Participation: Learning from Successful Reforms*, Getting Skills Right, OECD Publishing, Paris. [37]

OECD (forthcoming), *Monitoring participation in adults learning programmes*, OECD Publishing. [42]

O'Neill, S. and M. Thomson (2013), "Supporting academic persistence in low-skilled adult learners", *Support for Learning*, Vol. 28/4, pp. 162-172, http://dx.doi.org/10.1111/1467-9604.12038. [36]

Pareliussen, J. (2016), "Age, skills and labour market outcomes in Finland", *OECD Economics Department Working Papers*, No. 1321, OECD Publishing, Paris, https://dx.doi.org/10.1787/5jlv23953gq1-en. [4]

Pennacchia, J. et al. (2018), *Barriers to learning for disadvantaged groups*. [29]

Prime Minister's Office (2019), *Experimental Finland*, https://kokeilevasuomi.fi/en/key-project (accessed on 16 September 2019). [22]

Roosmaa, E. and E. Saar (2017), "Adults who do not want to participate in learning: a cross-national European analysis of their perceived barriers", *International Journal of Lifelong Education*, Vol. 36/3, pp. 254-277, http://dx.doi.org/10.1080/02601370.2016.1246485. [28]

Semmar, Y. (2006), "Distance Learners and Academic Achievement: The Roles of Self-Efficacy, Self-Regulation and Motivation", *Journal of Adult and Continuing Education*, Vol. 12/2, pp. 244-256, http://dx.doi.org/10.7227/jace.12.2.9. [11]

Steiner, M. et al. (2017), *Evaluation der Initiative Erwachsenenbildung*, Institut für Höhere Studien, Wien. [39]

Steuerungsgruppe Initiative Erwachsenenbildung (2019), *Programmplanungsdokument Initiative Erwachsenenbildung. Länder-Bund-Initiative zur Förderung grundlegender Bildungsabschlüsse für Erwachsene inklusive Basisbildung*, http://www.initiative-erwachsenenbildung.at. [40]

Sulkunen, S. and A. Malin (2018), "Literacy, Age and Recentness of Education Among Nordic Adults", *Scandinavian Journal of Educational Research*, Vol. 62/6, pp. 929-948, http://dx.doi.org/10.1080/00313831.2017.1324898. [7]

TAIKOJA (2019), *TAIKOJA*, https://taikoja.fi/. [25]

Tiina Korhonen (2018), *Regional Employment Trials*, MEE Finland, Helsinki. [26]

Tuomaala, M. (2018), "Aktiivisilta työvoimapoliittisilta palveluilta avoimille työmarkkinoille sijoittuminen", *TEM-analyyseja*, Vol. 88. [14]

Veronica McGivney (1993), "Participation and non-participation: a review of the literature", in Edwards, R., S. Sieminski and D. Zeldin (eds.), *Adult learners, education and trianing*, Routledge. [12]

Windisch, H. (2016), *How to motivate adults with low literacy and numeracy skills to engage and persist in learning: A literature review of policy interventions*, Springer Netherlands, http://dx.doi.org/10.1007/s11159-016-9553-x. [30]

Winsten, F. (2019), *Helsini Skills Centre - Competence ahead of education, professions and work*. [21]

Woessmann, L. (2016), "The economic case for education", *Education Economics*, Vol. 24/1, pp. 3-32, http://dx.doi.org/10.1080/09645292.2015.1059801. [1]